Channel Zero

By

Alwy M. Jones

Buy Me Coffee

Everything All Through All At The Same Time

Spinmeister

You see the mote in your brother's eye but
not the beam in your own eye.

Isa ibn Maryam (Jesus PBUH)

PREFACE

In an era where Western nations proudly champion themselves as bastions of human rights, democracy, and equality, a stark contradiction emerges between their lofty proclamations and the sobering reality within their own borders. Channel Zero seeks to critically examine the hypocrisy of Western countries regarding human rights, race equality, and civil rights, exposing the gap between their international advocacy and domestic failures. The concept of universal human rights, enshrined in the Universal Declaration of Human Rights, has long been a cornerstone of Western diplomatic rhetoric. Yet, as we delve deeper into the societal fabric of these nations, we uncover a troubling pattern of systemic discrimination, inequality, and rights violations that persist despite decades of purported progress.

From the United States to the United Kingdom and across Europe, Western countries have historically positioned themselves as global leaders in promoting human rights. However, their domestic records tell a different story. In the US, the legacy of slavery and segregation continues to cast a long shadow, manifesting in racial disparities across education, healthcare, criminal justice, and economic opportunity. The UK grapples with its colonial past while facing accusations of institutional racism within its police force and government institutions. Across Europe, the treatment of migrants and refugees often falls short of the human rights standards these nations advocate internationally.

The significance of addressing this hypocrisy cannot be overstated. As Western nations continue to wield considerable influence on the global stage, their credibility as human rights advocates is increasingly scrutinized. The disconnect between their external posturing and internal realities not only undermines their moral authority but also provides ammunition for authoritarian regimes to deflect criticism of their own human rights abuses. Moreover, this hypocrisy fuels cynicism and erodes public trust in the very concept of universal human rights, potentially jeopardizing decades of progress in this field.

Florida State Prison

Florida State Prison (FSP), located in Starke, Florida, was established in 1968 and is one of the state's most notorious correctional facilities. Originally built to house inmates in a maximum security environment, FSP has a capacity of approximately 1,500 inmates, although this number can fluctuate based on the prison's operational needs and inmate classification systems. The prison is known for housing some of Florida's most dangerous offenders, including those on death row. FSP features several notable programs aimed at rehabilitation, including educational and vocational training initiatives. These programs are designed to equip inmates with skills that can aid in their reintegration into society upon release. However, the effectiveness and accessibility of these programs have been subjects of ongoing debate.

The conditions within Florida State Prison have drawn significant scrutiny, particularly regarding the use of corporal punishment and prolonged isolation. Reports indicate that a substantial number of inmates are subjected to solitary confinement, often spending 22 to 24 hours a day in isolated cells. These cells are typically small, around nine by seven feet and feature solid steel doors with minimal light and ventilation.

Statistics reveal that as of recent reports, approximately 240 prisoners in Florida are held in solitary confinement, representing about one sixth of the total prison population. This rate is significantly higher than the national average. The implications of such isolation are severe, with many inmates experiencing detrimental psychological effects due to the lack of human interaction and sensory stimulation.

The psychological and physical effects of long term isolation are well documented. Studies indicate that inmates subjected to solitary confinement often experience heightened levels of anxiety, depression, and other mental health issues. 91% reported experiencing anxiety, 70% felt an impending nervous breakdown and 86% experienced oversensitivity to stimuli.

Moreover, the physical health consequences can be equally alarming; prolonged isolation has been linked to increased rates of heart palpitations and other stress related conditions. Experts argue that these conditions can lead to a cycle of mental illness that complicates rehabilitation efforts and increases recidivism rates among former inmates.

The legal framework surrounding corporal punishment and isolation practices in Florida prisons has been contentious. The use of solitary confinement raises significant ethical questions regarding human rights and the treatment of incarcerated individuals. Advocacy groups have called for investigations into the overuse of solitary confinement in Florida, arguing that it violates the Civil Rights of Institutionalized Persons Act (CRIPA).

Controversies have arisen over incidents where inmates have died or suffered severe health consequences while in solitary confinement, prompting calls for reform from human rights organizations. Legal challenges have also emerged, questioning whether such practices constitute cruel and unusual punishment under the Eighth Amendment.

Alabama Department of Corrections

The Alabama Department of Corrections (ADOC) has faced significant scrutiny in recent years due to a range of systemic issues, including overcrowding, violence, inadequate medical care, and high rates of homicide and sexual abuse. Alabama's prison system is currently grappling with severe overcrowding. The prison population exceeded 25,000 inmates, which is approximately 7,000 over the design capacity. This situation has persisted since at least 2016, when overcrowding was first highlighted as a critical issue. The state's prisons are designed to hold around 19,000 inmates, yet they often operate at 190% of their intended capacity.

Historical trends indicate that overcrowding has worsened over the years due to various factors, including increased sentencing lengths and a lack of effective parole systems. For example, despite a recommended parole grant rate of 80% based on scoring formulas, actual grants have plummeted to as low as 5% in recent months. This disparity has been attributed to stricter requirements imposed by the Alabama Board of Pardons and Paroles, which has led to a backlog of inmates serving lengthy sentences without the possibility of early release. The implications of overcrowding are dire; it exacerbates violence within prisons, strains resources, and compromises inmate welfare. Reports have indicated that inmates are often housed in unsanitary conditions with insufficient access to basic necessities.

Violence within Alabama's prisons has reached alarming levels. A report revealed that assaults in state prisons increased by more than 41% compared to the previous year, with a total of 2,073 recorded assaults; 1,578 being inmate on inmate incidents and 495 involving assaults on staff. This surge in violence highlights the dangerous environment created by overcrowded conditions and inadequate staffing. Many facilities operate with significantly fewer correctional officers than needed to maintain order. The influx of weapons and drugs exacerbates tensions and leads to violent confrontations. Staff often lack proper training to manage conflicts effectively or de-escalate volatile situations. The increase in violence has prompted federal investigations into the ADOC's practices and conditions, revealing systemic failures that leave inmates vulnerable to harm.

Healthcare services within Alabama's correctional facilities have been described as "horrendously inadequate." A federal court ruling emphasized that mental health care is particularly lacking, leading to a skyrocketing suicide rate among inmates. The court found that prisoners with serious mental health needs often go untreated or are disciplined for behaviors stemming from their illnesses. There are not enough medical professionals available to meet the needs of the inmate population. Many facilities lack adequate medical facilities or resources. Reports have surfaced detailing instances where inmates received insufficient care for serious medical conditions. Health outcomes for inmates reflect these deficiencies; studies have shown that mortality rates in Alabama prisons are significantly higher than national averages. For example, between 2008 and 2014, the mortality rate in Alabama's prisons more than doubled.

Alabama's rates of homicide and sexual abuse within its correctional facilities are among the highest in the nation. The state recorded over 34 homicides per 100,000 incarcerated individuals, which is more than 600% greater than the national average from 2001 to 2014. The Equal Justice Initiative reported that between 2008 and 2014 alone, there were 35 murders across various ADOC facilities. Sexual abuse is another pressing issue; many inmates report experiencing sexual violence at the hands of both fellow inmates and staff members. The prevalence of such incidents raises serious concerns about safety and inmate rights within the prison system.

Guantanamo Bay Detention Camp

The Guantanamo Bay detention camp was established in January 2002 by the Bush administration in response to the September 11th 2001 terrorist attacks. Located on the U.S. Naval Base in Guantanamo Bay, Cuba, the facility was designed to hold individuals suspected of involvement in terrorism, particularly those captured during the War on Terror in Afghanistan and elsewhere. Initially, the camp's purpose was to detain and interrogate high value suspects associated with al-Qaeda and the Taliban. The first detainees arrived on January 11th 2002, and at its peak, the facility held approximately 780 prisoners. The Bush administration argued that these detainees were "enemy combatants" who did not qualify for protections under the Geneva Conventions, a stance that would later face significant legal challenges.

The detention camp quickly became a focal point for human rights concerns. Many detainees were held indefinitely without charge or trial, raising issues of arbitrary detention and violations of international law. Human rights organizations and legal experts argued that this practice contradicted fundamental principles of due process and the rule of law. Reports of torture and inhumane treatment emerged, including allegations of waterboarding, sleep deprivation, and other "enhanced interrogation techniques". These practices not only violated international laws against torture but also had severe psychological impacts on detainees. Many prisoners reportedly developed mental health issues due to prolonged isolation and harsh treatment. The lack of fair trial processes was another significant concern. The military commissions established to try detainees were criticized for falling short of international standards for fair trials. Many detainees were held for years without being charged or brought before a court, violating basic principles of justice.

The experiences of Guantanamo detainees have been marked by prolonged detention, isolation, and uncertainty. Some individuals have been held for over two decades without trial. This extended detention has had profound effects on their mental health and well-being. One notable case is that of Khalid Sheikh Mohammed, alleged mastermind of the 9/11 attacks, who has been held at Guantanamo since 2006 without a trial date set. Such cases highlight the complex legal and ethical issues surrounding the detention camp. Many detainees have reported experiencing severe psychological distress, including anxiety, depression, and post-traumatic stress disorder. The isolation from family and the outside world, combined with the uncertainty of their legal status, has exacerbated these mental health challenges.

The Guantanamo detention camp has faced numerous legal challenges over the years. In a series of landmark decisions, the U.S. Supreme Court ruled that detainees have the right to challenge their detention in federal courts (Rasul v. Bush, 2004) and that the military commissions as initially constituted were illegal (Hamdan v. Rumsfeld, 2006)

Politically, the camp has been a subject of intense debate. While some argue for its necessity in combating terrorism, others view it as a violation of human rights and a stain on America's international reputation. Various administrations have grappled with the challenge of closing the facility, with President Obama signing an executive order in 2009 to close Guantanamo, though this goal remained unfulfilled.

Rikers Island

Rikers Island, a 413 acre facility located in the East River between Queens and the Bronx, serves as one of the most infamous jails in the United States. Established in 1932, it has become a critical component of New York City's correctional system, housing pretrial detainees and those serving short sentences. Historically, Rikers has been plagued by issues ranging from overcrowding and violence to inadequate mental health care, raising significant concerns about the treatment of its inmates and the overall efficacy of the correctional system.

Since 2014, Rikers Island has experienced fluctuating inmate populations, with significant spikes in overcrowding. In 2014, the average daily population was around 10,000 inmates. However, this number has dropped to approximately 5,600, largely due to ongoing reforms aimed at reducing incarceration rates. Despite this reduction, Rikers remains over capacity; the facility was designed to hold about 4,000 inmates, indicating a persistent issue with overcrowding.

The causes of overcrowding at Rikers are multifaceted. A reliance on cash bail has led to many individuals being incarcerated pretrial simply because they cannot afford bail. Lengthy sentences for non-violent offenses contribute to a backlog in the system. The lack of effective diversion programs for non-violent offenders exacerbates the situation.

The impact of overcrowding on inmate welfare is profound. Overcrowded conditions lead to increased tension among inmates and staff, reduced access to essential services like healthcare and mental health support, and heightened risks of violence. Furthermore, inmates often experience inadequate living conditions, including unsanitary environments and insufficient access to basic necessities.

Violence at Rikers Island is a significant concern, manifesting in various forms including inmate on inmate assaults and staff on inmate brutality. Reports indicate that violence has surged over recent years; for instance, incidents of serious violence reportedly increased by 50% from 2019 to 2021. A troubling pattern has emerged where violent incidents often involve gang activity or retaliation against perceived slights. The sheer number of inmates creates an environment ripe for conflict. Gangs operate within the facility, often exerting control over other inmates and contributing to violent confrontations.

Mental health care at Rikers Island is severely lacking. Approximately 55% of the inmate population has a documented mental illness, with around 20% suffering from serious mental health disorders requiring intensive care. Despite this high prevalence, access to adequate mental health services remains limited.

From 2014 to present, there has been a troubling trend regarding mental health issues among inmates. Reports indicate that there were over 500 instances of suicide attempts or self-harm within just six months in 2023. At least 18 deaths related to mental health crises have occurred since 2020.

High suicide rates among inmates point to systemic failures in providing necessary support. Many individuals are left untreated for their conditions due to staffing shortages and logistical challenges within the facility.

San Quentin State Prison

San Quentin State Prison, located in Marin County, California, is the oldest prison in the state, having opened in 1854. Originally established to house male inmates, it has gained notoriety as the only prison in California that conducts executions. Over the years, San Quentin has housed many infamous inmates, including Charles Manson and Sirhan Sirhan. The prison has a population of approximately 3,500 inmates, significantly exceeding its designed capacity of around 2,200. This overcrowding has led to numerous systemic issues affecting inmate welfare and prison operations.

San Quentin's inmate population has fluctuated dramatically over the years. In 2014, the average daily population was around 4,000, but efforts to reduce incarceration rates have led to a gradual decrease. Despite this reduction, the facility remains critically overcrowded. The current population of approximately 3,500 still represents a significant strain on resources and infrastructure. California's "three strikes" law and mandatory minimum sentences for certain crimes have resulted in longer incarceration periods for many inmates. The lack of effective diversion programs for non-violent offenders contributes to higher incarceration rates. High recidivism rates further exacerbate overcrowding as individuals cycle in and out of the prison system.

Overcrowded facilities lead to unsanitary conditions, increased tension among inmates, and reduced access to essential services such as healthcare and mental health support. The lack of space and resources can escalate conflicts among inmates, leading to higher rates of violence within the facility.

There have been numerous reports and documented cases of excessive use of force by guards at San Quentin. In 2017, an inmate was severely beaten by guards during a cell extraction, resulting in multiple injuries. The incident was captured on video and led to public outcry. A 2020 report highlighted a pattern of excessive force used against inmates during routine interactions, with several cases resulting in serious injuries.

Some guards faced disciplinary actions; however, many cases resulted in minimal consequences. Legal actions have been taken against the state by advocacy groups seeking accountability for the abusive treatment of inmates. A high staff to inmate ratio can lead to increased tensions and reliance on force to maintain control. A longstanding culture within some correctional facilities normalizes excessive force as an acceptable means of control.

Pelican Bay State Prison

Pelican Bay State Prison (PBSP), located in Crescent City, California, is one of the most notorious correctional facilities in the United States. Opened in 1989, it was designed to house California's most dangerous criminals, particularly those involved in gang related activities. The prison is notable for its Security Housing Unit (SHU), which is specifically intended for inmates deemed too dangerous to be housed in the general population. With a current population of approximately 3,500 inmates, including over 1,000 in solitary confinement, Pelican Bay serves as a critical focal point for discussions surrounding the ethics and efficacy of long term isolation as well as the adequacy of mental health care provided to inmates.

As of 2023, Pelican Bay houses over 1,000 inmates in its SHU. These inmates are subjected to extreme isolation conditions, spending nearly 23 hours a day locked in windowless cells measuring approximately 8 by 10 feet. Inmates typically have limited access to outdoor exercise; often confined to a small concrete yard for just five hours per week.

From 2012 to the present, many inmates have remained in solitary confinement for extended periods. Reports indicate that some individuals have spent over 10 years in the SHU, with an average duration exceeding four years. This prolonged isolation can lead to severe psychological effects and has raised concerns about the long term consequences of such treatment.

Numerous studies have documented the detrimental effects of long term solitary confinement on mental health. Research indicates that inmates subjected to prolonged isolation often experience; severe anxiety and depression, hallucinations, paranoia and increased risk of self-harm and suicide. A study conducted by the American Psychological Association found that individuals in solitary confinement are at significantly higher risk for developing mental health disorders compared to those housed in general population settings. Experts argue that these conditions can amount to cruel and unusual punishment, violating the Eighth Amendment of the U.S. Constitution.

Pelican Bay State Prison does provide some mental health services; however, these services are often criticized as inadequate. Inmates have access to mental health evaluations and treatment; yet, staffing shortages and high inmate to therapist ratios hinder effective care delivery. The inadequacy of mental health services can have dire consequences. In 2020, an inmate committed suicide after reportedly being denied timely access to mental health support. A case study highlighted an inmate who developed severe depression after spending over a decade in solitary confinement without adequate psychological intervention.

International human rights organizations have condemned long-term solitary confinement practices as forms of torture. The United Nations' Standard Minimum Rules for the Treatment of Prisoners (the Nelson Mandela Rules) emphasize that prolonged isolation should be avoided due to its harmful effects on mental health. Human rights advocates argue that the treatment of inmates at Pelican Bay raises serious ethical questions about rehabilitation versus punishment. Critics contend that subjecting individuals to extreme isolation undermines any potential for rehabilitation and reintegration into society.

Tutwiler Prison for Women

Tutwiler Prison for Women, located in Wetumpka, Alabama, is one of the most notorious correctional facilities for women in the United States. Established in 1942, it was designed to house female inmates convicted of various offenses. Over the years, however, Tutwiler has gained infamy due to its alarming rates of sexual abuse and harassment perpetrated by staff members against inmates. With a population that fluctuates around 1,000 women, the prison has become a focal point for discussions surrounding the treatment of incarcerated women and the systemic issues that facilitate abuse. The environment at Tutwiler Prison is characterized by inadequate facilities and a lack of oversight that contributes to a culture of abuse. The prison's design includes limited privacy for inmates, with blind spots that allow staff to exploit their positions. Policies regarding staff prisoner interactions are often poorly enforced, leading to a toxic atmosphere where sexual misconduct can thrive.

Reports indicate that male staff members frequently have access to areas where female inmates are undressing or using the restroom, creating opportunities for voyeurism and harassment. The prison's management has been criticized for failing to implement effective training and oversight mechanisms that could mitigate these risks.

From 2010 onward, numerous documented incidents of sexual abuse and harassment have emerged from

Tutwiler Prison. According to a report from the Equal Justice Initiative (EJI), Tutwiler has consistently ranked among the highest facilities in the nation for sexual assault against women inmates. In 2012, EJI published findings detailing widespread sexual violence at Tutwiler, including cases where female inmates became pregnant after being raped by correctional officers. These findings were corroborated by interviews with over fifty current and former inmates. Victims of abuse often face severe psychological trauma, compounded by punitive responses from prison officials when they report misconduct. Many women have reported being placed in segregation or facing retaliation for speaking out about their experiences.

A 2014 report from the U.S. Department of Justice found that Tutwiler had one of the highest rates of sexual abuse in women's prisons nationwide. Between 2009 and 2011, six correctional officers were convicted for criminal sexual abuse against incarcerated women at Tutwiler; however, only one received a significant sentence.

The Alabama Department of Corrections (ADOC) has faced significant scrutiny regarding its handling of allegations of sexual abuse at Tutwiler. Following EJI's complaint in 2012, the U.S. Justice Department launched an investigation into the conditions at Tutwiler, which confirmed widespread abuse. In 2015, a federal lawsuit resulted in a settlement requiring ADOC to implement reforms aimed at protecting inmates from sexual violence. These reforms included improved reporting mechanisms for allegations and increased oversight.

State Correctional Institution Greene

State Correctional Institution (SCI) Greene, located in Waynesburg, Pennsylvania, is a high security prison primarily housing male inmates convicted of serious offenses. Established in 1996, SCI Greene has become significant within the Pennsylvania correctional system due to its role in managing violent offenders and its reputation for strict security measures. However, the institution has faced serious allegations of staff misconduct, particularly regarding physical abuse against inmates. SCI Greene was designed to house a maximum security population and has a capacity of approximately 1,800 inmates. The facility's population hovers around 1,600, indicating a relatively stable inmate count. The staff to inmate ratio is reported at about 1:4, which can lead to challenges in monitoring inmate interactions and maintaining order.

Historically, SCI Greene has faced scrutiny for various operational practices. Previous investigations have highlighted issues related to inadequate training for staff and insufficient oversight mechanisms that could prevent misconduct. In 1998, for example, a significant investigation into inmate abuse led to disciplinary actions against multiple staff members. Despite these past incidents, reports of physical abuse have persisted over the years.

Numerous allegations of physical abuse by staff members at SCI Greene have emerged; in June 2018 an inmate reported being beaten by several correctional officers during a cell extraction. The inmate alleged that officers used excessive force, resulting in injuries that required medical attention. In March 2019, a group of inmates filed complaints stating that they were subjected to physical violence during a routine lockdown. Witnesses reported seeing officers strike inmates while they were restrained. In November 2020 a former inmate testified that he was assaulted by guards after he attempted to report misconduct. He described being thrown to the ground and kicked multiple times. Inmates have consistently reported a culture of fear within SCI Greene, where retaliation for reporting abuse is common. One inmate stated, "If you say anything, you'll be punished worse than before."

In response to specific complaints, state police conducted an investigation into the alleged use of excessive force by correctional officers. The Pennsylvania Department of Corrections (DOC) initiated its own internal investigation into staff conduct at SCI Greene.

Corcoran State Prison

Corcoran State Prison, located in the arid landscape of California's Central Valley, is a maximum security facility that has gained notoriety for its controversial practices and violent incidents. Opened in 1988, Corcoran was designed to house some of the state's most dangerous criminals. However, it has also become infamous for allegations of excessive force by guards, particularly through organized inmate fights that have been likened to gladiatorial contests.

Corcoran State Prison was established in response to California's growing prison population during the 1980s. The facility was built to accommodate approximately 3,000 inmates and has been known for housing high profile inmates, including notorious gang members and violent offenders. Over the years, however, Corcoran has faced numerous controversies regarding inmate treatment and staff conduct.

Since its opening, Corcoran has been the site of several significant events that have drawn attention to its operational practices. In 1996 Riot a deadly riot broke out at the prison, resulting in one inmate's death and highlighting severe management issues. In the early 1990s, it was revealed that guards were orchestrating fights between inmates as a form of entertainment.

Corcoran houses approximately 2,500 inmates, with a staff to inmate ratio that raises concerns about adequate supervision and oversight.

Numerous allegations have surfaced regarding excessive force used by guards at Corcoran. In 2017 Incident an inmate reported being beaten by multiple guards during a cell extraction. The inmate claimed he was restrained and punched repeatedly while on the ground. In a 2019 Testimony, a former inmate recounted witnessing guards kick an inmate who was already subdued. "They just kept hitting him," he said. "It was like they were trying to prove a point." These testimonies illustrate a troubling pattern of behavior among some staff members at Corcoran. Many inmates report experiencing anxiety, depression, and post-traumatic stress disorder (PTSD) as a result of their treatment. Physical injuries sustained from assaults can lead to long term health issues.

The phenomenon of gladiator style fights at Corcoran involves guards allegedly facilitating or encouraging fights between rival gangs or inmates for entertainment. Reports indicate that these fights were often organized with little regard for inmate safety.

Whistleblowers and former inmates have provided chilling accounts of these events. One former guard stated, "It was like watching a dogfight. The guards would place bets on who would win." Another inmate described how fights were often coerced; "If you didn't fight, you'd get punished worse."

These accounts reveal a disturbing culture within the prison where violence is not only tolerated but actively promoted by those in charge.

Broward Correctional Institution

Broward Correctional Institution (BCI), located in Fort Lauderdale, Florida, was established in 1977 as a facility primarily for female inmates. Over the years, it has served various purposes within the Florida Department of Corrections, including housing female death row inmates until 2003. At its peak, BCI had a capacity of approximately 624 inmates, primarily focusing on rehabilitation and reintegration programs for women. However, the institution faced numerous challenges, including allegations of abusive practices and inadequate medical care, leading to its closure in 2012.

The use of handcuffs as a form of punishment at BCI has been a contentious issue. Inmates reported that handcuffs were frequently used during disciplinary actions, often without justification. The policies surrounding their use were vague, allowing staff considerable discretion in applying restraints. Reports indicate that between 2010 and 2012, there were numerous documented incidents where inmates were placed in handcuffs for extended periods as a punitive measure. An internal review in 2011 revealed that over 30% of inmates reported being handcuffed during routine interactions with staff. In one notable incident, an inmate was handcuffed for six hours without access to basic needs after a verbal altercation with a guard. Such practices not only raise ethical concerns but also highlight the psychological impact on inmates.

Broward Correctional Institution struggled with overcrowding issues. Although the prison was officially closed due to declining crime rates and reduced prison admissions, reports indicated that it often operated near or above capacity prior to its closure.

Numerous reports have highlighted the inadequate medical care provided to inmates at BCI. Advocacy groups raised concerns about the quality and accessibility of healthcare services within the facility. A report by the Florida Commission on Offender Review indicated that over 40% of inmates reported delays in receiving medical attention. Testimonies from former inmates reveal alarming accounts of neglect. One inmate described waiting weeks for treatment for a severe infection.

Sde Teiman

Sde Teiman, an Israeli military facility located in the Negev Desert near the Gaza Strip, has gained notoriety as a detention camp for Palestinians. Originally a military base, it was repurposed to accommodate detainees under the Unlawful Combatants Law, allowing for prolonged detention without charge. This facility has been described as "Israel's Guantanamo" due to the severe allegations of human rights abuses reported within its confines.

Numerous allegations have surfaced regarding torture, sexual abuse, and inhumane treatment at Sde Teiman. Testimonies from released detainees reveal harrowing accounts of mistreatment. Detainees report being subjected to physical abuse, including beatings with metal batons and gun butts, electric shocks during interrogations, and positional torture where they are forced into painful positions for extended periods. Disturbingly, testimonies include accounts of rape and sexual violence perpetrated by both male and female guards. One released detainee described being gang raped while restrained, highlighting a pattern of sexual violence that has emerged in multiple reports. Detainees have also reported experiences of sensory deprivation through blindfolding and prolonged isolation, coupled with verbal humiliation and threats. These accounts have been corroborated by whistleblower testimonies from Israeli personnel who worked at the facility, further validating claims of systemic abuse.

The situation at Sde Teiman has drawn significant attention from international human rights organizations and bodies such as the United Nations. Various UN experts have condemned the use of torture at Sde Teiman as a violation of international law. They have characterized the practices observed there as potential crimes against humanity. Reports from B'Tselem and the Association for Civil Rights in Israel (ACRI) detail systemic abuse within Israeli detention facilities. B'Tselem's report titled "Welcome to Hell" documents testimonies from 55 released Palestinian detainees who describe their experiences of torture and ill treatment. ACRI highlights a staggering lack of accountability within the Israeli justice system, noting that out of nearly 1,500 torture complaints filed over two decades, there have been virtually no indictments.

Investigations into the allegations at Sde Teiman are ongoing, but progress has been slow. Recent incidents have prompted some governmental responses; however, skepticism remains regarding the military judiciary's ability to impartially address these claims amidst political pressures. Activists continue to call for accountability and transparency in both military and civilian courts to ensure that abuses are addressed adequately.

Ofer Prison

Ofer Prison, officially known as Incarceration Facility 385, is a significant Israeli detention center located near Ramallah in the occupied West Bank. Established in 1988 during the First Intifada, it has become a focal point of tension in the Israeli-Palestinian conflict. The prison, now under the control of the Israel Prison Service (IPS), can hold up to 800 prisoners, including both tried individuals and those under administrative detention. Reports from former detainees and human rights organizations paint a grim picture of the living conditions within Ofer Prison. Overcrowding is a persistent issue, with cells designed for six inmates often housing up to twelve. Detainees describe inadequate provision of basic necessities; insufficient bedding, with only six beds and thin blankets for twelve inmates, limited access to restroom facilities, restricted outdoor time, often as little as 15 minutes twice a week and meager food rations, with reports of shared yogurt and single vegetables among multiple prisoners. The physical environment is reportedly harsh, particularly during winter months when detainees struggle with cold temperatures due to lack of proper clothing and blankets.

Numerous allegations of torture and mistreatment have emerged from Ofer Prison. Former detainees have reported frequent beatings by guards, often without provocation, forced degrading practices, such as being made to shout "thank you, Captain" in

Hebrew, denial of medical care and psychological abuse, including threats and humiliation. These practices reportedly intensified following the October 2023 conflict escalation, with National Security Minister Itamar Ben Gvir openly advocating for harsher treatment of Palestinian detainees. The use of solitary confinement in Ofer Prison has been a subject of particular concern. While specific details about its implementation in Ofer are limited in the provided sources, solitary confinement is generally used as a punitive measure or for alleged security reasons. The psychological impact of this practice can be severe, potentially leading to long term mental health issues for detainees.

The conditions and practices at Ofer Prison have raised significant human rights concerns. International organizations and human rights groups argue that these practices violate several international laws and conventions, including; the UN Convention against Torture, the International Covenant on Civil and Political Rights and the Fourth Geneva Convention. Of particular concern is the treatment of minors in the facility. Non-governmental organizations have reported the imprisonment of children in Ofer, with allegations of handcuffing and the use of iron shackles on minors, practices considered in breach of the UN Convention on the Rights of the Child.

Recent reports indicate a worsening of conditions since October 2023. The number of Palestinians held by the IPS has increased from around 5,500 to approximately 9,000 as of January 2024, including dozens of minors and women. Nearly one third of those in custody are held under administrative detention, a practice that allows indefinite detention without charge or trial. Efforts to challenge these conditions through Israeli courts have so far been unsuccessful, and attempts to engage the medical community in safeguarding detainees' right to adequate care have also failed.

Megiddo Prison

Megiddo Prison, located in northern Israel near the city of Afula, is one of the country's main facilities for the detention of Palestinian prisoners. Established in the early 1980s, it serves as a high security prison primarily for individuals convicted of security offenses, including those related to the Israeli-Palestinian conflict. The significance of human rights violations within this prison extends beyond its walls, reflecting broader issues of systemic abuse and neglect within Israel's detention system. The documented cases of physical abuse, intimidation tactics, and systemic torture practices reported at Megiddo Prison raise critical questions about the treatment of detainees and Israel's adherence to international human rights standards.

Megiddo Prison was established during a period of heightened tension between Israelis and Palestinians, particularly following the First Intifada in the late 1980s. Over the years, it has housed thousands of Palestinian detainees, many held under administrative detention without formal charges. The prison's design and operational policies have evolved, but reports of abuse and mistreatment have persisted.

In Israel, the treatment of prisoners is governed by both domestic laws and international conventions. The Israeli Penal Law and the Prisons Ordinance set out regulations for prisoner treatment. However, numerous reports indicate that these laws are frequently violated, particularly concerning Palestinian detainees.

HaMoked, an Israeli human rights organization, has documented numerous cases of physical abuse at Megiddo Prison. Detainees have recounted incidents where they were physically assaulted by prison guards using batons and other implements. Testimonies describe guards entering cells to beat prisoners without provocation. There are alarming accounts of dogs being used to intimidate detainees. For instance, one former prisoner described being forced to kneel while a guard unleashed a dog on him as a form of psychological torture. These cases highlight a pattern of violence that raises serious concerns about the treatment of detainees at Megiddo. Detainees often experience psychological abuse through verbal humiliation and threats. This includes threats of sexual violence and other forms of intimidation aimed at instilling fear. The implications of these practices extend beyond immediate physical harm; they can lead to long term psychological effects such as PTSD and anxiety disorders among detainees.

Russian Compound (al-Maskoubiyeh) In Jerusalem

The Russian Compound, known in Arabic as al-Maskoubiyeh, is a historically significant site located in central Jerusalem. Established between 1860 and 1864, it was initially built to accommodate Russian Orthodox pilgrims visiting the Holy Land. The compound includes several notable structures, most prominently the Cathedral of the Holy Trinity, which was consecrated in 1872. The complex served various functions over the years, including housing a consulate, a hospital, and hostels for pilgrims.

Historically, the Russian Compound reflects the broader context of Russian imperial ambitions in the region during the 19th century. The Imperial Orthodox Palestine Society played a crucial role in its establishment, promoting religious and cultural ties between Russia and Jerusalem. Over time, the compound transitioned into a governmental and administrative hub under British Mandate rule and later became associated with Israeli security forces following the establishment of Israel in 1948.

Reports from former detainees and human rights organizations have detailed severe allegations of physical abuse and humiliation during interrogations at the Russian Compound. Former detainees have described being subjected to brutal beatings by interrogators. One individual recounted an incident where he was repeatedly struck while blindfolded, resulting in severe injuries. Interrogation methods reportedly include degrading practices such as forced nudity, verbal abuse, and threats of sexual violence. These tactics are designed to instill fear and compliance among detainees. These accounts have been corroborated by human rights organizations that advocate for accountability regarding these abuses.

Conditions within the Russian Compound have been characterized as degrading and abusive by former detainees and human rights advocates. The facility often operates beyond its intended capacity, leading to cramped conditions. Detainees have expressed concerns about insufficient access to medical care for injuries sustained during interrogations or due to poor living conditions. Reports indicate that requests for medical attention are often ignored or delayed. The combination of physical abuse, overcrowding, and lack of adequate care contributes to significant mental health issues among detainees, including anxiety disorders and depression.

The continued reports of torture at the Russian Compound highlight systemic issues within Israel's detention practices. Human rights organizations such as B'Tselem and the Public Committee Against Torture in Israel (PCATI) have documented numerous allegations. According to PCATI's reports, there have been over 1,500 documented cases of torture complaints lodged against Israeli security forces since 2001; however, very few have led to investigations or accountability for perpetrators.

Reports indicate that torture is not an isolated incident but rather part of a broader pattern observed across various detention facilities in Israel. This systemic issue raises serious concerns about compliance with international human rights standards.

Experts argue that existing laws governing prisoner treatment are inadequately enforced. The absence of independent oversight mechanisms allows abuses to persist without accountability. Israeli authorities have largely dismissed allegations of abuse as politically motivated or exaggerated. This stance undermines efforts to address human rights violations within the detention system.

Damon Prison

Damon Prison, located near Haifa, Israel, is a facility primarily housing Palestinian detainees, including women. The prison has garnered attention due to reports of severe human rights violations and deteriorating conditions, particularly in the wake of recent escalations in the Israeli-Palestinian conflict. The significance of prison conditions in relation to human rights cannot be overstated; they reflect a country's commitment to justice and the humane treatment of all individuals, regardless of their legal status.

Allegations of sexual violence against female detainees at Damon Prison have been documented by organizations such as B'Tselem and Amnesty International. Reports indicate that female detainees have faced threats of sexual violence during their arrest and detention. For instance, testimonies reveal instances where detainees were threatened with rape by officers during interrogations. Specific cases highlight the psychological trauma inflicted on women who endure not only physical abuse but also the constant fear of sexual violence in an environment designed to punish and control.

Claims regarding inadequate medical care for detainees at Damon Prison are alarming. Reports suggest that many inmates suffer from untreated medical conditions due to insufficient access to healthcare services. Vulnerable populations, particularly women who may require specific medical attention related to reproductive health, are disproportionately affected by these deficiencies. The lack of timely medical treatment can lead to severe health implications, exacerbating existing conditions and contributing to long term physical and mental health issues among inmates.

The treatment of detainees at Damon Prison has been characterized by harsh conditions that include physical and psychological abuse. Reports indicate that detainees experience frequent beatings, humiliation, and degrading treatment as part of their daily lives within the facility. Such actions violate international human rights standards, which prohibit torture and cruel treatment. The systematic nature of these abuses reflects a broader pattern within Israeli detention practices that undermine the dignity and rights of Palestinian prisoners.

The harsh conditions at Damon Prison have profound impacts on inmates' mental and physical health. Many detainees report experiencing anxiety, depression, and post-traumatic stress disorder as a result of their treatment. Families of inmates also suffer as they face uncertainty regarding their loved ones' well-being, often enduring emotional distress due to lack of communication or information about their health status. The ripple effects extend into communities, where the stigma associated with incarceration can lead to social isolation and economic hardship.

Ashkelon Prison

Ashkelon Prison, located in southern Israel, is known for housing Palestinian detainees, including those accused of security offenses. The facility has been a focal point for numerous allegations of torture and mistreatment, particularly in light of the recent escalation in hostilities and the subsequent increase in detainee numbers. These allegations raise serious concerns regarding the treatment of inmates and adherence to international human rights standards.

Reports from various human rights organizations detail numerous allegations of torture within Ashkelon Prison. Detainees have claimed that food is often withheld as a form of punishment. For instance, testimonies indicate that prisoners may receive only one meal a day, with water being similarly restricted to exert control over them. Allegations include beatings by prison guards, often occurring during transfers or interrogations. Reports suggest that detainees are subjected to severe physical violence, including being kicked, punched, and beaten with batons. Inmates have reported being blindfolded and handcuffed for extended periods, subjected to psychological games designed to instill fear and submission. This includes threats of sexual violence and humiliation. Credible sources such as reports from the UN Special Rapporteur on Torture and various human rights organizations document these allegations extensively. For example, a recent report highlighted systematic abuse by Israeli Prison Service officers against

Palestinian prisoners, including instances where detainees were kept in degrading conditions and subjected to violence.

Many former detainees report experiencing long-term mental health issues such as anxiety, depression, and post-traumatic stress disorder (PTSD). The trauma from physical abuse and psychological torture can lead to lasting emotional scars. Inmates often suffer from untreated injuries due to the lack of proper medical care. Testimonies reveal that some detainees endure severe pain from previous beatings without access to necessary medical treatment.

The current state of overcrowding within Ashkelon Prison exacerbates the mistreatment of inmates. Reports indicate that the prison is operating beyond its capacity, leading to increased tensions among detainees and staff. Recent developments have seen Israeli officials acknowledging the overcrowding issue but proposing punitive measures rather than reforms. National Security Minister Itamar Ben Gvir has suggested reducing inmate rights further as a solution to overcrowding, which raises alarms about potential escalations in mistreatment. This approach reflects a troubling trend where conditions are downgraded under the guise of security measures.

The absolute prohibition against torture is enshrined in various treaties, including the Convention Against Torture (CAT), which Israel is obligated to uphold.

Ktzi'ot Prison

Ktzi'ot Prison, located in the Negev Desert approximately 45 miles southwest of Beersheba, is Israel's largest detention facility by land area. Originally established during the First Intifada, it has a long history of housing Palestinian detainees, including those held under administrative detention without formal charges. The prison has become a focal point for allegations of torture and mistreatment, particularly in light of recent escalations in the Israeli-Palestinian conflict. The detainees at Ktzi'ot Prison predominantly include Palestinians accused of security offenses, often captured during military operations or protests. Many are held under administrative detention, which allows for indefinite imprisonment without trial. This context sets the stage for serious human rights concerns regarding their treatment during interrogations and throughout their incarceration.

Numerous allegations of torture have emerged from Ktzi'ot Prison, with former detainees recounting harrowing experiences during their time in custody. Detainees have described being beaten with batons and subjected to severe physical violence during interrogations. Some accounts detail instances where guards would enter cells and indiscriminately beat inmates, often targeting sensitive areas such as the head and genitals. Psychological torture methods reportedly include threats of sexual violence and humiliation. Detainees have recounted being stripped naked and forced into degrading positions while being verbally abused by prison staff. Reports indicate that detainees are often denied basic necessities such as food and water as a form of punishment. For instance, one former inmate described being limited to just one hour of water per day for multiple prisoners, leading to dire sanitary conditions.

Testimonies from former detainees provide chilling insights into these practices. Mohammed Al-Bazz, who spent time in Ktzi'ot after being arrested in 2023, described a particularly traumatic incident where guards stripped prisoners naked and urinated on them while subjecting them to physical beatings.

The living conditions within Ktzi'ot Prison have been characterized by overcrowding, inadequate sanitation, and insufficient access to food and medical care. Reports indicate that Ktzi'ot is often overpopulated, with many prisoners crammed into small cells designed for fewer occupants. Detainees have reported unsanitary conditions, including a lack of proper hygiene facilities. The spread of diseases such as scabies has been noted among inmates due to poor living conditions and inadequate medical attention. Allegations suggest that food rations are frequently insufficient, with some prisoners receiving only one meal a day. Access to clean water is also severely restricted, leading to further health complications. Human rights organizations such as B'Tselem have documented these conditions extensively, noting that they violate both Israeli law and international human rights standards.

The Central Park Five

In the late 1980s, New York City was grappling with a surge in crime, largely attributed to the crack cocaine epidemic. This period was marked by heightened racial tensions, economic disparity, and a growing fear of violence, particularly in urban areas. The city was often portrayed as a battleground, where crime rates soared and public safety became a pressing concern for residents and officials alike.

On the night of April 19th 1989, Trisha Meili, a 28 year old white female jogger, was brutally attacked in Central Park. She was found unconscious and severely injured, having been raped and beaten. The assault left her in a coma for twelve days and sparked widespread media coverage and public outrage. During this time, numerous reports of "wilding"; a term used to describe groups of teenagers engaging in violent behavior circulated, further inflaming racial tensions and fears within the community.

In the aftermath of Meili's attack, police apprehended five teenagers; Antron McCray (15), Kevin Richardson (14), Yusef Salaam (15), Raymond Santana (14), and Korey Wise (16). They were taken into custody based on their presence in Central Park that evening and alleged involvement in other crimes reported during the same time frame. The police quickly focused on these boys as suspects in Meili's assault.

The interrogations that followed were marked by coercive tactics. The teenagers were subjected to hours of intense questioning without legal representation or parental guidance. Under psychological pressure and fear of further consequences, they provided confessions that were inconsistent and factually inaccurate. These confessions were later recanted, with the boys claiming they had been coerced into admitting guilt.

Despite the lack of physical evidence linking them to the crime, such as DNA evidence that did not match any of the boys, the confessions formed the cornerstone of the prosecution's case. The trials of the Central Park Five took place in a highly charged atmosphere influenced by media sensationalism and racial bias. The prosecution relied heavily on the coerced confessions while ignoring significant evidence that contradicted their claims. The media portrayed the defendants as dangerous criminals, exacerbating public sentiment against them.

Ultimately, all five teenagers were convicted on charges including assault and robbery. Korey Wise received the longest sentence as he was tried as an adult, resulting in a prison term of up to fifteen years; the others received sentences ranging from five to ten years in juvenile detention.

In 2002, Matias Reyes, a convicted serial rapist serving time for other crimes, confessed to attacking Meili. His detailed account matched evidence from the crime scene, including DNA that confirmed his sole responsibility for the assault. This revelation prompted a re-examination of the case against the Central Park Five.

On December 19th 2002, Justice Charles J. Tejada vacated the convictions based on Reyes' confession and supporting DNA evidence. This decision marked a significant turning point for the exonerated men who had endured years of wrongful imprisonment.

The Central Park Five were targeted largely due to their race and socioeconomic status. The tactics used during interrogations raised questions about the validity of confessions obtained under duress. Sensationalist reporting contributed to public hysteria and shaped perceptions that undermined fair legal processes.

The Central Park Five case has had a profound influence on discussions surrounding race and justice in America. It has been referenced in various media representations, including documentaries like Ken Burns' "The Central Park Five" and Netflix's "When They See Us," which have brought renewed attention to issues of wrongful convictions and systemic racism within law enforcement.

Anthony Ray Hinton

Anthony Ray Hinton was born on June 1st 1956, in Alabama. He grew up in a modest household and worked at a supermarket warehouse, living with his mother in rural Alabama. In 1985, Hinton's life took a tragic turn when he was wrongfully arrested for the murders of two fast food restaurant managers in Birmingham, Alabama. His case would eventually highlight significant flaws within the American criminal justice system.

On February 25th and July 2nd 1985, John Davidson and Thomas Wayne Vason, two fast food restaurant managers, were killed during armed robberies. The police investigation initially yielded no suspects until a survivor of a third robbery identified Hinton from a photo lineup. Despite his alibi; working at a locked warehouse fifteen miles away during the time of the murders, Hinton was arrested. The prosecution's case hinged on an old revolver belonging to Hinton's mother, which they claimed was used in the murders based on ballistics evidence.

Hinton faced two counts of capital murder for the deaths of Davidson and Vason. The prosecution's case was built primarily on ballistics evidence that claimed bullets found at the crime scenes matched Hinton's mother's revolver. Notably, there were no eyewitnesses or fingerprint evidence linking him to the crimes.

The trial began in 1986 and was marred by significant issues regarding the reliability of the ballistics evidence. The state's expert testified that the bullets matched Hinton's mother's gun; however, this conclusion was later challenged by independent forensic experts who stated that the evidence was inconclusive. Unfortunately, Hinton's defense attorney failed to secure a competent firearms expert, instead hiring someone with limited expertise who was visually impaired and unable to properly analyze the evidence. The jury convicted Hinton in just one hour with a 10-2 vote; Alabama law allows non-unanimous verdicts for death penalty cases despite compelling evidence of his innocence and a polygraph test that indicated he did not commit the crimes.

In 2015, after nearly three decades on death row, the U.S. Supreme Court unanimously ruled that Hinton had received ineffective legal representation during his trial. The Court found that his attorney had failed to seek adequate funding for a qualified ballistics expert to challenge the prosecution's claims effectively. This ruling was crucial not only for Hinton's case but also highlighted broader issues regarding inadequate legal counsel in capital cases.

The Supreme Court's decision underscored systemic flaws within the death penalty system, particularly concerning how inadequate legal representation can lead to wrongful convictions. It raised awareness about the importance of competent defense attorneys in capital cases and prompted discussions about reforming legal standards for death penalty cases nationwide.

In April 2015, after new ballistics tests were conducted that excluded Hinton as a suspect, he was finally released from prison. The tests confirmed that the bullets from the crime scenes could not have been fired from his mother's gun. On April 3rd 2015, he walked out of Jefferson County Jail as a free man after spending nearly 30 years on death row.

Following his exoneration, Hinton became an advocate against the death penalty and for criminal justice reform. He published a memoir titled "The Sun Does Shine: How I Found Life and Freedom on Death Row", which details his experiences and reflections on justice and humanity. He has traveled extensively to share his story and raise awareness about wrongful convictions and systemic injustices within the legal system.

Hinton's case has significantly impacted public awareness regarding flaws in the death penalty system. His story exemplifies how racial bias, inadequate legal representation, and unreliable forensic evidence can lead to devastating miscarriages of justice.

Kalief Browder

Kalief Browder was born on May 25th 1993, in the Bronx, New York City, into a challenging socio-economic environment. He was the youngest of three siblings raised by his mother, Venida Browder, in a neighborhood plagued by poverty and violence. The family faced numerous hardships, and Kalief struggled with the pressures of growing up in a community where crime was prevalent. Despite these challenges, he was known for his playful personality and interests in video games and wrestling.

At the age of 16, Kalief's life took a devastating turn when he was arrested for allegedly stealing a backpack. His story became emblematic of the failures within the criminal justice system, particularly regarding the treatment of young people and the use of pretrial detention.

On May 15th 2010, Kalief Browder was stopped by police while walking home from a party. He was accused of robbing a man two weeks earlier who claimed that Browder had stolen his backpack. The accusation was based on inconsistent statements from the accuser and did not include any physical evidence linking Browder to the crime. Despite this lack of evidence, he was arrested and charged with robbery, grand larceny, and assault.

Kalief maintained his innocence throughout the process and refused to accept plea deals that would have allowed him to avoid jail time but required him to admit guilt. His steadfastness would lead to a prolonged legal battle that would change his life forever.

Browder's incarceration at Rikers Island began immediately after his arrest. He spent nearly three years in this notorious facility without ever being convicted of a crime. During this time, he faced severe conditions. His case was delayed over 28 times due to various prosecutorial requests for postponements, which contributed to his extended stay without trial. Kalief spent more than 700 days in solitary confinement; a practice widely criticized for its psychological impact, where he was confined to a small cell for 23 hours a day. Reports indicated that Browder suffered physical abuse at the hands of both inmates and guards. Surveillance footage captured instances where he was beaten by officers. The combination of these factors created an environment that severely impacted his mental health and well-being.

The conditions at Rikers Island took a significant toll on Kalief's mental health. After enduring years of trauma, including multiple suicide attempts during his incarceration, Kalief developed severe depression and anxiety. The experiences he faced in solitary confinement and the violence he witnessed contributed to lasting psychological scars. Upon release, he struggled with flashbacks and feelings of paranoia. Kalief's mother noted that despite being physically free after his release in 2013, her son remained mentally imprisoned by his experiences at Rikers Island.

In 2013, after nearly three years behind bars, the charges against Kalief were finally dropped due to lack of evidence when the accuser failed to appear in court. Following his release, Kalief attempted to rebuild his life; he earned his GED and enrolled in community college. However, the psychological impact of his incarceration lingered. Despite efforts to move forward, such as receiving support from an anonymous donor who paid for his college tuition, Kalief continued to struggle with mental health issues. Tragically, on June 6th 2015, just two years after his release, Kalief took his own life at the age of 22.

Kalief Browder's story resonated deeply within American society and served as a catalyst for discussions about systemic issues within the criminal justice system. Browder's inability to secure bail set at $3,000 reflected broader issues within New York's bail system that disproportionately affected low income individuals. His prolonged detention without trial raised urgent questions about pretrial practices and their implications for justice. The use of solitary confinement for juveniles became a focal point for advocacy groups seeking reform.

John Thompson

John Thompson was born on March 25th 1962, in New Orleans, Louisiana. He grew up in a challenging environment marked by poverty and crime, which shaped his early experiences. By the time he reached adulthood, Thompson was a father trying to support his two children through various means, including small time drug dealing. His life took a tragic turn in 1984 when he became embroiled in a murder case that would lead to nearly three decades of wrongful imprisonment.

On March 2nd 1984, the body of 29 year old J. Michael Liuzza was discovered in New Orleans. He had been shot multiple times, and the police quickly focused their investigation on Thompson after he was implicated by a witness who claimed to have seen him near the crime scene. The circumstances surrounding the murder were murky, and Thompson's connection to the crime was tenuous at best. Thompson's trial began in 1985, and it was fraught with significant issues. The prosecution presented several pieces of evidence against him, including witness testimonies and circumstantial evidence. However, the case relied heavily on the credibility of witnesses who were often unreliable.

Crucially, evidence that could have exonerated Thompson was suppressed by the prosecution. This included blood evidence from the crime scene that did not match Thompson's blood type. Prosecutors had conducted tests that identified the perpetrator's blood type as "B," while Thompson's blood type was "O." This critical information was never disclosed to Thompson's defense team. Thompson's defense strategy also faltered significantly. His public defender failed to present key witnesses who could have provided alibis or cast doubt on the reliability of the prosecution's witnesses. The lack of a robust defense contributed to Thompson's conviction for murder and subsequent sentencing to death.

In 1986, John Thompson was sentenced to death for Liuzza's murder. The implications of this sentence were profound; he spent nearly 29 years in prison, with 14 of those years on death row at Angola Prison, a facility notorious for its harsh conditions. Living under the constant threat of execution took an immense psychological toll on Thompson, as he grappled with fear and despair while fighting for his life.

In 2009, after years of legal battles and advocacy from various organizations, DNA evidence emerged that would ultimately clear John Thompson. Investigators uncovered the suppressed blood evidence that had been hidden by prosecutors during his trial. This evidence conclusively proved that Thompson could not have been the murderer. The exoneration process involved legal challenges and a retrial based on newly discovered evidence. In September 2009, after nearly three decades behind bars, Thompson was finally declared innocent and released from prison. The emotional and psychological effects of his wrongful conviction were profound; while he regained his freedom, he struggled with the trauma of his experience.

Following his exoneration, John Thompson filed a lawsuit against the Orleans Parish District Attorney's Office for failing to disclose exculpatory evidence that violated his constitutional rights. The lawsuit highlighted systemic issues within the prosecutorial practices in New Orleans. Thompson's legal team argued that there was a culture of misconduct within the district attorney's office under Harry Connick Sr., which fostered an environment where evidence suppression was commonplace. In 2011, a jury awarded Thompson $14 million in damages for his wrongful conviction; one million dollars for each year he spent on death row.

However, this victory was short lived; in 2013, the U.S. Supreme Court ruled against Thompson in Connick v. Thompson, stating that Connick could not be held liable for failing to train prosecutors adequately regarding their obligations under Brady v. Maryland. This decision underscored how systemic issues can persist even when individual cases reveal egregious misconduct.

The Tuskegee Syphilis Study

The Tuskegee Syphilis Study, officially known as the "Tuskegee Study of Untreated Syphilis in the Negro Male," was a notorious medical research project conducted by the U.S. Public Health Service (PHS) from 1932 to 1972. Its primary purpose was to observe the natural progression of untreated syphilis in African American men, particularly to determine whether the disease had different effects based on race. This study took place against a backdrop of systemic racism, social inequality, and a lack of access to healthcare for African Americans, particularly in the rural South.

During the early 20th century, the United States was marked by Jim Crow laws that enforced racial segregation and discrimination. African Americans were often denied basic rights and faced significant barriers to healthcare. The Tuskegee Study exploited these vulnerabilities, targeting impoverished black men from Macon County, Alabama, many of whom were sharecroppers with little education and limited understanding of medical practices.

One of the most egregious aspects of the Tuskegee Syphilis Study was the complete neglect of informed consent. Participants were not informed that they had syphilis; instead, they were misled into believing they were receiving treatment for "bad blood," a local term that encompassed various ailments, including anemia and fatigue.

The ethical implications of this deception are profound. The participants were never made aware of their diagnosis or the fact that effective treatment, specifically penicillin, became widely available in the late 1940s. Despite this knowledge, researchers deliberately withheld treatment from the men involved in the study, violating their rights and autonomy as individuals.

The health consequences for participants in the Tuskegee Study were severe and often tragic. Many men suffered from advanced stages of syphilis without any medical intervention. The untreated disease led to numerous complications. Syphilis can cause damage to the heart and blood vessels. Untreated syphilis can lead to neurosyphilis, resulting in severe mental health problems and cognitive decline. It is estimated that more than 100 participants died from complications related to tertiary syphilis during the course of the study. The impact on individual lives was devastating, with many participants experiencing debilitating health issues that could have been avoided with appropriate treatment.

The long term effects of the Tuskegee Syphilis Study extended beyond physical health complications; they also affected families and communities. The stigma associated with syphilis contributed to social isolation for many participants. Additionally, because some men transmitted the disease to their partners, families faced further repercussions.

Documented cases indicate that several deaths attributed to untreated syphilis occurred during the study's duration. These deaths underscored not only personal tragedies but also a broader failure of medical ethics and responsibility.

The legacy of the Tuskegee Syphilis Study has had lasting repercussions on African American communities' trust in medical institutions. The study is often cited as a prime example of medical racism and unethical research practices. This betrayal has fostered a deep seated skepticism towards healthcare systems among African Americans, influencing how they perceive medical research and treatment today.

The Guatemala Syphilis Experiment

The Guatemala Syphilis Experiment, conducted between 1946 and 1948, stands as one of the most egregious examples of unethical medical research in history. This experiment involved the deliberate infection of over 1,300 individuals with sexually transmitted diseases (STDs) such as syphilis, gonorrhea, and chancroid, without their informed consent. The study aimed to assess the effectiveness of penicillin in treating these infections and to explore other potential treatments. The significance of this study lies not only in its scientific objectives but also in its profound implications for medical ethics and public health practices.

The Guatemala Syphilis Experiment occurred during a period marked by significant social and political upheaval. Following World War II, the United States was navigating complex relationships with Latin American countries while grappling with issues related to race, class, and medical ethics. In this context, the U.S. Public Health Service (USPHS) sought to conduct research that would inform public health strategies for controlling STDs among military personnel and the general population.

Syphilis is a sexually transmitted infection caused by the bacterium Treponema pallidum. By the mid-20th century, penicillin had emerged as an effective treatment for syphilis, drastically reducing morbidity associated with the disease. However, its use was not universally understood, particularly regarding its prophylactic capabilities. Researchers were interested in exploring whether penicillin could prevent infection after exposure to syphilis and other STDs.

The primary objective of the Guatemala Syphilis Experiment was to evaluate the effectiveness of penicillin in preventing syphilis after exposure. To achieve this, researchers employed a variety of methods to infect subjects intentionally. Participants included a diverse group of vulnerable individuals; prisoners, sex workers, soldiers, psychiatric patients, and orphans. Many were from marginalized communities in Guatemala, making them particularly susceptible to exploitation. The selection process lacked ethical rigor; subjects were often unaware that they were part of a medical experiment.

One of the most troubling aspects of the experiment was the absence of informed consent. Participants were not informed about their syphilis diagnosis or that they were being deliberately infected with STDs. This violation of ethical standards has had lasting repercussions on trust between medical institutions and marginalized communities.

The health consequences for those involved in the Guatemala Syphilis Experiment were severe. Many participants suffered from untreated syphilis and other STDs, leading to significant health complications such as neurological damage, cardiovascular issues, and even death.

While some findings related to penicillin's effectiveness were documented, they came at an enormous human cost. Of the approximately 5,500 individuals involved in various aspects of the study, at least 83 died by 1953; however, it remains unclear how many deaths can be directly attributed to the infections inflicted during the study.

In 2010, U.S. President Barack Obama issued a formal apology to Guatemalan President Álvaro Colom for the actions taken during the experiment.

Aboriginal Pain Experiments

The 1920s and 1930s in Australia were marked by significant socio-political turmoil, particularly concerning Aboriginal Australians. Following the colonization of Australia, Indigenous peoples faced systemic discrimination and marginalization. The prevailing attitudes during this period were heavily influenced by scientific racism, a belief that justified the superiority of certain races over others through pseudoscientific methods. This ideology was prevalent among researchers and policymakers, who often viewed Aboriginal Australians as inferior and in need of "civilizing."

The Stolen Generations policy, which involved the forcible removal of Aboriginal children from their families to assimilate them into white society, further exemplified the racial attitudes of the time. Aboriginal Australians were often depicted as a "dying race," leading to a sense of urgency among researchers to study them before they supposedly disappeared. This context laid the groundwork for unethical medical practices, including the Aboriginal Pain Experiments conducted by scientists from the University of Adelaide.

The primary objective behind the Aboriginal Pain Experiments was to study pain responses and physical measurements among Aboriginal Australians. Researchers, including physiologist Cedric Stanton Hicks, aimed to explore physiological differences purportedly linked to race. The experiments were driven by a desire to validate existing scientific theories that suggested racial differences in pain perception and other physical attributes. These motivations were steeped in a broader framework of eugenics, which sought to improve the genetic quality of populations based on flawed understandings of heredity and race. The experiments often involved invasive procedures designed to elicit pain responses, with little regard for the well-being of participants. Researchers operated under a misguided belief that such studies would yield valuable insights into human physiology, reinforcing their preconceived notions about racial superiority.

A critical ethical issue surrounding these experiments was the complete lack of informed consent. Participants were often recruited without any clear understanding of what the experiments entailed or the risks involved. Many Aboriginal individuals were coerced into participation through manipulation or exploitation, reflecting a profound disregard for their autonomy and rights. In many cases, researchers did not provide adequate information about the nature of the experiments or obtain consent from participants or their families. This practice violated fundamental ethical principles that prioritize respect for persons and their right to make informed decisions regarding their participation in research.

The methodologies employed in the Aboriginal Pain Experiments were invasive and often brutal. Researchers used various techniques to measure pain responses, including physical restraint and apparatuses that restricted breathing. For example, participants were required to lie still for extended periods while their physiological responses were recorded under distressing conditions.

Hicks noted that cooperation from subjects was difficult to obtain, often requiring physical coercion or manipulation. Descriptions from researchers indicated a lack of empathy towards participants, who were treated more like lab animals than human beings. The conditions under which these experiments were conducted were frequently harsh and dehumanizing. The psychological trauma inflicted upon participants was profound. Many individuals experienced lasting emotional distress due to their treatment during these experiments. Reports indicate that subjects suffered not only from physical pain but also from feelings of humiliation and degradation. Specific cases highlight the extent of harm inflicted on individuals. For instance, some participants became severely ill due to the invasive nature of the procedures they underwent. The long term effects included chronic health issues and psychological scars that persisted long after the experiments concluded.

Project MK Ultra

Project MK Ultra, initiated by the CIA in 1953, emerged during a period of intense geopolitical tension known as the Cold War. This era was characterized by fear of communism and concerns over the potential for Soviet advancements in mind control technologies. The CIA was particularly motivated by reports of Soviet and Chinese techniques used on American prisoners of war, which fueled paranoia within the agency regarding the need for effective countermeasures. The project was part of a broader strategy to enhance U.S. intelligence capabilities and psychological warfare. Directed by Sidney Gottlieb, MK Ultra operated under the auspices of national security, receiving substantial funding without significant oversight. It encompassed numerous subprojects aimed at developing methods for controlling human behavior, particularly for interrogation purposes. The clandestine nature of the program meant that many participants were unwitting subjects in a series of unethical experiments that would later be condemned for their disregard for human rights and ethical standards.

The methodologies employed in Project MK Ultra were diverse and often disturbing, involving a range of psychological and pharmacological techniques. One of the most notorious aspects was the administration of LSD, a powerful hallucinogen, to unwitting subjects. The CIA sought to explore how LSD could alter perceptions, induce compliance, or even wipe memories. In addition to LSD, various other drugs were tested to assess their effects on behavior and cognition. Electroshock Therapy was employed to induce confusion and trauma in subjects. Researchers experimented with hypnosis as a means to manipulate behavior. Subjects were also isolated from sensory input to explore its effects on mental states.

Specific experiments included administering LSD to mental patients, prisoners, and marginalized individuals such as sex workers; groups deemed vulnerable and unable to resist participation. For instance, one infamous case involved dosing a mental patient with LSD for an extended period without consent, leading to severe psychological distress.

The ethical violations inherent in Project MK Ultra are profound and troubling. The use of unwitting subjects directly contravened the principles of informed consent established by the Nuremberg Code following World War II. Participants were often unaware they were part of an experiment, raising serious moral questions about autonomy and human rights.

Many subjects reported chronic mental health issues stemming from their involvement in experiments. Some individuals developed PTSD due to the distressing nature of the experiments. The manipulative techniques used in many experiments led to profound disruptions in self-perception and identity among participants.

The Zo'e Tribe And Missionaries (1982-1987)

The Zo'e tribe, an indigenous group residing in the remote Amazon rainforest of northern Brazil, is known for its distinctive cultural practices and traditional way of life. Before contact with outside groups, the Zo'e lived in relative isolation, maintaining their customs, language, and social structures largely untouched by external influences. Their society revolved around hunting, fishing, and subsistence agriculture, with a deep spiritual connection to their environment.

During the early 1980s, Brazil was undergoing significant socio-political changes, including the expansion of missionary activities among indigenous populations. The Brazilian government had previously established policies aimed at protecting isolated tribes, but the interest of various missionary organizations, particularly the New Tribes Mission (Missao Novas Tribos do Brasil), began to challenge these protections. The missionaries sought to convert indigenous peoples to Christianity and introduce Western lifestyles, often disregarding the implications for tribal cultures.

The primary objective of the missionaries from New Tribes Mission was to convert the Zo'e to Christianity. They aimed to achieve this through a three stage process; learning the Zo'e language, initiating literacy programs, and translating the Bible into their language. The missionaries believed that by converting the Zo'e, they could save their souls and improve their living conditions through Western education and values.

However, these intentions carried significant cultural implications for the Zo'e community. The introduction of Christianity often came with the imposition of foreign values that conflicted with traditional beliefs. The missionaries viewed their work as a moral imperative, yet this perspective failed to recognize the autonomy of the Zo'e and their right to maintain their cultural identity. As a result, the Zo'e faced pressure to abandon their traditional practices in favor of new religious beliefs and lifestyles. The contact between the Zo'e and missionaries had immediate and devastating consequences. One of the most critical issues was exposure to new diseases. Prior to contact, the Zo'e had little to no immunity against common illnesses such as influenza and malaria. As missionaries entered their territory and interacted with them, these diseases spread rapidly among the tribe.

Moreover, there was a glaring lack of informed consent regarding this contact. The Zo'e were not fully aware of the risks involved in interacting with outsiders or how their lives would change as a result. This disregard for their autonomy raises ethical concerns about the responsibilities of outsiders engaging with indigenous communities.

Following initial contact, medical care provided to the Zo'e was inadequate. Although some medical assistance was offered by missionaries and later by FUNAI (Brazil's National Indian Foundation), it often came too late or was insufficient to address the health crises that emerged.

The most notable epidemics included outbreaks of malaria and influenza, which decimated the population. Reports indicate that approximately 45 Zo'e died between 1987 and 1991 due to these diseases, significantly impacting their community dynamics. The mortality rates associated with these outbreaks highlighted not only the vulnerability of isolated tribes but also the ethical implications of introducing outside influences without adequate health protections in place.

The contact with missionaries profoundly disrupted traditional lifestyles among the Zo'e. Their health practices rooted in centuries of knowledge about local flora and fauna were undermined as they began relying on external medical interventions that did not align with their cultural practices. Social structures also shifted as a result of outside influence. Traditional roles within families and communities were challenged by new religious teachings and practices introduced by missionaries. The Zo'e experienced changes in their cultural practices; for instance, communal activities centered around hunting and gathering were affected as some members began to adopt Western goods and lifestyles offered by missionaries.

Cuba

In 1962, Cuba found itself at the center of Cold War tensions between the United States and the Soviet Union. Following Fidel Castro's rise to power in 1959, Cuba rapidly aligned itself with the Soviet bloc, embracing communist ideology and forging close economic and military ties with Moscow. This shift in allegiance alarmed the United States, which viewed Cuba's proximity as a potential threat to national security. The Cuban Missile Crisis of October 1962 further exacerbated tensions, as the Soviet Union attempted to place nuclear missiles on Cuban soil. This event brought the world to the brink of nuclear war and solidified Cuba's position as a key player in the Cold War geopolitical landscape.

One of the primary catalysts for U.S. sanctions against Cuba was the widespread nationalization of American owned properties and businesses by the Castro regime. In 1960, Cuba began expropriating U.S. assets; oil refineries owned by Esso, Texaco, and Shell, the Cuban Telephone Company, 36 sugar mills and Compania Cubana de Electricidad (Cuban Electric Company). These nationalizations were estimated to be worth over $1 billion in 1960 dollars, representing a significant loss for American investors.

Cuba's growing alliance with the Soviet Union significantly influenced U.S. foreign policy decisions. The Eisenhower administration viewed this partnership as a direct threat to U.S. interests in the Western Hemisphere. The fear of communist expansion in Latin America, coupled with Cuba's strategic location just 90 miles from Florida, led to a hardening of U.S. policy towards the island nation.

The U.S. embargo against Cuba, initiated in 1962, comprises a complex set of economic sanctions; a ban on all exports to Cuba, with exceptions for food and medicine, prohibition of U.S. citizens from engaging in financial transactions with Cuba, restrictions on travel to Cuba by U.S. citizens and freezing of Cuban government assets in the United States. In addition to economic sanctions, the United States severed diplomatic relations with Cuba in January 1961. This action effectively isolated Cuba from its largest neighbor and historical trading partner.

The sanctions have had a profound and lasting impact on the Cuban economy and its people. Estimated economic losses of approximately $130 billion over six decades. Severe shortages of essential goods, including food and medicine. Restricted access to modern medical equipment and treatments.

The long term effects of the sanctions have led to limited economic opportunities and high unemployment rates, chronic shortages leading to malnutrition and disease outbreaks and a particularly severe "Special Period" in the 1990s following the collapse of the Soviet Union, characterized by extreme economic hardship.

Economic Sanctions On Iraq (1990-2003)

In August 1990, following Iraq's invasion of Kuwait, the United Nations Security Council imposed comprehensive economic sanctions on Iraq through Resolution 661. These sanctions, initially intended to pressure Iraq to withdraw from Kuwait, remained in place for over a decade after the Gulf War ended, lasting until 2003. The sanctions regime had profound and far reaching consequences for the Iraqi civilian population, leading to a humanitarian crisis of unprecedented scale. The sanctions imposed on Iraq were among the most comprehensive ever implemented. They prohibited all imports and exports with Iraq, with only narrow exemptions for medicine and, in humanitarian circumstances, foodstuffs. The enforcement mechanisms effectively blocked Iraq from importing food, despite its reliance on imports for 70% of its food supply at the time. The sanctions were further intensified after the Gulf War through Resolution 687, which included provisions for the removal of weapons of mass destruction. The UN took complete control over the Iraqi economy, depriving the country of sovereignty over its trade.

The impact of the sanctions on Iraq's economy was swift and severe. Within a year of their imposition, Iraq's exports plummeted by 97%, and imports declined by 90%. The prohibition on oil exports during the initial five years of sanctions deprived Iraq of its primary source of hard currency, leading to a severe devaluation of the currency and rampant inflation. By 1995, the value of the Iraqi dinar had depreciated by 5,000%, resulting in an average monthly income equivalent to just two US dollars. Food prices skyrocketed by 4,500%, and households' purchasing power was reduced to only 5% of what it had been before August 1990.

The economic collapse led to widespread malnutrition among the Iraqi population. In 1993, the UN's World Food Program and the Food and Agriculture Organization reported that the sanctions had caused "persistent deprivation, severe hunger and malnutrition for a vast majority of the Iraqi population". By 1997, UNICEF noted that 31% of children under the age of five suffered from malnutrition. In 2000, a UNICEF official informed the 661 Committee that 25% of children in south and central governorates suffered from chronic malnutrition, which was often irreversible, and 9% from acute malnutrition.

The sanctions had a devastating impact on Iraq's healthcare system. The country was left with only one fully functioning X-ray machine by 1999, and long forgotten diseases returned. The complex licensing requirements effectively prevented food, medicine, and medical equipment from reaching Iraqis. The education system also suffered greatly. As state revenues dwindled and wages lost their value, over 12,000 teachers resigned. The lack of resources and the overall economic hardship led to a significant decline in educational standards and opportunities for Iraqi children. The sanctions, combined with the damage from the Gulf War, led to a severe breakdown of Iraq's infrastructure. Water and sanitation systems were particularly affected. The destruction of water treatment facilities and the lack of resources for maintenance led to widespread contamination of water sources, contributing to the spread of waterborne diseases.

UNICEF reports indicated that child mortality rates doubled in the decade following the imposition of the sanctions. It is estimated that approximately 500,000 excess child deaths could be attributed to the sanctions. This staggering figure underscores the severe humanitarian cost of the sanctions on the most vulnerable members of Iraqi society.

Sanctions Imposed On Iran

The history of sanctions against Iran dates back to 1979, following the Iranian Revolution and the subsequent hostage crisis at the U.S. Embassy in Tehran. On November 14th 1979, President Jimmy Carter signed Executive Order 12170, freezing approximately $12 billion in Iranian assets, including bank deposits, gold, and other properties. This marked the beginning of a long standing sanctions regime against Iran. The initial sanctions were primarily a response to the hostage crisis, but over the years, they evolved to address broader concerns, including Iran's nuclear program, support for international terrorism, and human rights violations. While some sanctions were lifted after the hostages' release in 1981, new ones were imposed in 1984 when the U.S. State Department designated Iran as a state sponsor of terrorism.

A significant escalation in sanctions began in 2010, following Iran's continued pursuit of its nuclear program. The United Nations Security Council, the United States, and the European Union all imposed new, more comprehensive sanctions. On June 9th 2010, the UN Security Council adopted Resolution 1929, which tightened proliferation related sanctions on Iran. This was followed by the U.S. Comprehensive Iran Sanctions, Accountability, and Divestment Act on June 24th, and the European Union's targeted sanctions on July 26th 2010.

The sanctions imposed on Iran encompass a wide range of restrictions, primarily focusing on economic, financial, and trade aspects. These include bans on imports and exports, particularly targeting Iran's oil and gas sector. For instance, in 2012, the European Union agreed to ban imports of Iranian oil. Financial Sanctions target Iranian banks and financial institutions, including the Central Bank of Iran, aiming to isolate Iran from the international financial system and restrict its ability to conduct transactions in foreign currencies. Trade Restrictions prohibited the sale of certain goods and technologies to Iran, especially those that could be used in its nuclear program or military applications. Travel Bans and Asset Freezes targeted specific individuals and entities associated with Iran's nuclear program or human rights violations. The UN imposed an arms embargo on Iran, which expired in October 2020 as per the terms of the 2015 nuclear deal.

The sanctions against Iran have been ongoing for over four decades, making them one of the longest standing and most comprehensive sanctions regimes in modern history. Despite brief periods of easing, such as during the implementation of the Joint Comprehensive Plan of Action (JCPOA) in 2015, the core of the sanctions has remained in place since 1979.

The prolonged sanctions have had severe consequences for Iran's civilian population. Iran's economy has experienced significant contraction, with high inflation rates severely impacting purchasing power. By 1995, the value of the Iranian rial had depreciated by 5,000%, resulting in an average monthly income equivalent to just two US dollars. There have been persistent shortages of essential goods, including food and medicine. Despite exemptions for humanitarian goods, the complexity of the sanctions regime has deterred many companies from engaging in any trade with Iran. The economic downturn has led to increased poverty rates and high unemployment, particularly among youth. Iranian businesses and individuals face significant challenges in conducting international transactions, affecting trade and personal finances. The severe devaluation of the Iranian rial has made imported goods prohibitively expensive for many Iranians, affecting their quality of life and access to essential products.

One notable example of the sanctions' impact is the reported shortage of essential medicines in 2019, particularly for cancer treatment. Despite exemptions for humanitarian goods, the complex nature of the sanctions and fear of potential repercussions led many pharmaceutical companies to cease business with Iran. This resulted in severe shortages of crucial medications, directly affecting public health and the treatment of serious illnesses.

The Ferguson Protests

On August 9th 2014, Michael Brown, an unarmed 18 year old African American, was shot and killed by Ferguson police officer Darren Wilson in Ferguson, Missouri. The incident occurred after Brown was stopped for walking in the street with a friend, Dorian Johnson. Initially suspected of theft related to a convenience store incident earlier that day, the encounter escalated into a confrontation that ended with Wilson firing twelve shots at Brown, hitting him six times. Witness accounts varied; some claimed Brown had his hands raised in surrender when he was shot, while others supported Wilson's narrative of a struggle. Ferguson is a predominantly Black suburb of St. Louis, characterized by its socioeconomic challenges and a history of racial tensions between the police and the community. The shooting sparked outrage and protests, as many residents felt that Brown's death was emblematic of broader issues of systemic racism and police brutality in the United States.

Following Brown's death, protests erupted in Ferguson, initially starting as peaceful demonstrations but quickly escalating into more intense confrontations with law enforcement. The protests began on August 10th 2014, and continued for several weeks. The demonstrators included a diverse demographic mix of local residents, activists from across the country, and members of various civil rights organizations. Many protesters adopted the slogan "Hands up, don't shoot!" as a rallying cry against police violence. The protests drew national attention and became a focal point for discussions about race relations in America. As tensions rose, the situation escalated into clashes between protesters and law enforcement, leading to instances of violence and property damage.

The response from law enforcement during the Ferguson protests was heavily criticized for its militarized approach. Officers deployed tear gas and rubber bullets against demonstrators, which many viewed as excessive force. Eyewitness accounts described scenes of chaos as police used armored vehicles and military grade equipment to disperse crowds.

One protester recalled; "It felt like we were in a war zone... they were firing tear gas at us like we were criminals." The aggressive tactics employed by the police not only intensified the protests but also fueled public outrage regarding police conduct. The events surrounding the Ferguson protests raised serious allegations of police brutality. Many protesters reported experiencing excessive force from law enforcement officers during demonstrations. Accounts included instances of physical assaults and unwarranted detentions. The aggressive tactics used by police contributed to a growing mistrust between the community and law enforcement agencies. Public perception shifted dramatically as many began to view the police not as protectors but as aggressors against their own community.

In response to the events in Ferguson, several legal actions were initiated against the Ferguson Police Department (FPD). Michael Brown's family filed a wrongful death lawsuit against the city, which resulted in a $1.5 million settlement in 2017. Additionally, various civil rights organizations filed complaints highlighting systemic issues within the FPD. The legal scrutiny prompted discussions about police accountability and led to calls for reforms within law enforcement agencies nationwide.

In light of the events in Ferguson, the U.S. Department of Justice launched an investigation into the practices of the Ferguson Police Department. The findings released in March 2015 revealed significant patterns of racial bias within the department's policing practices. The DOJ report highlighted that African Americans were disproportionately targeted for stops and arrests compared to their white counterparts. It also documented instances where officers used excessive force without justification. The report criticized not only individual officers but also systemic issues within the department that perpetuated discrimination.

The Family Separation Policy At The U.S.-Mexico Border

In April 2018, the Trump administration announced a "zero tolerance" immigration policy, which mandated the criminal prosecution of all individuals caught entering the United States illegally, including those seeking asylum. This policy led to the systematic separation of migrant families at the U.S.-Mexico border, as children could not be held in criminal detention facilities with their parents. The political context surrounding this policy was characterized by the Trump administration's hardline stance on immigration. The stated goal was to deter illegal border crossings and address what the administration perceived as a crisis at the southern border. However, this approach marked a significant departure from previous practices, where families were generally kept together during immigration proceedings.

The scale of family separations was substantial. Between mid-April and early June 2018, more than 2,000 children were separated from their parents. By 2021, it was estimated that the policy had affected approximately 5,500 children. The psychological impact on both children and parents was severe. Many children experienced trauma, anxiety, and depression as a result of being separated from their caregivers. Parents reported feelings of helplessness, guilt, and profound distress. Mental health experts warned of the long-term consequences of such separations, particularly on young children's development and emotional well-being.

Human rights organizations and legal experts raised serious concerns about the policy. They argued that it violated international human rights laws, including the right to family unity and the principle of non-refoulement, which prohibits returning asylum seekers to countries where they may face persecution. The policy faced widespread condemnation both nationally and internationally. The United Nations High Commissioner for Human Rights called it "unconscionable," and several countries, including the United Kingdom and Canada, publicly criticized the practice.

Numerous lawsuits were filed against the federal government in response to the family separations. One of the most significant was Ms. L v. ICE, filed by the American Civil Liberties Union (ACLU) in February 2018. This lawsuit led to a federal court order in June 2018 that halted family separations and mandated the reunification of separated families. The court ruling required the government to reunite children under five with their parents within 14 days and older children within 30 days. However, the government struggled to meet these deadlines due to inadequate record keeping and the complexity of the reunification process.

Racial Discrimination In Healthcare

Systemic racism in healthcare refers to the ingrained policies, practices, and norms within the healthcare system that disadvantage racial and ethnic minority groups. This form of racism is often subtle and operates through institutional structures rather than overt discrimination, leading to significant disparities in health outcomes. One of the most alarming manifestations of this systemic issue is the disparity in maternal mortality rates between Black women and white women in the United States. Black women are disproportionately affected by high maternal mortality rates, highlighting a critical area where systemic racism continues to impact health equity.

Maternal mortality is defined as the death of a woman during pregnancy or within 42 days of termination of pregnancy, irrespective of the duration or site of the pregnancy. According to recent data, Black women are three times more likely to die from pregnancy related complications than white women. This stark difference underscores the urgent need to address the underlying factors contributing to these disparities.

Recent statistics illustrate the significant gap in maternal mortality rates between Black and white women. As of 2021, the maternal mortality rate for Black women was approximately 55.3 deaths per 100,000 live births compared to 19.1 deaths per 100,000 live births for white women. A report from MBRRACE-UK indicated a fourfold increase in maternal mortality rates among Black women between 2019 and 2021, while rates for Asian women doubled during the same period. Research published in Health Affairs highlighted that systemic factors such as access to care, socioeconomic status, and implicit bias among healthcare providers contribute significantly to these disparities. These statistics reveal not only a troubling trend but also a systemic failure to provide equitable care.

The demographic affected by these disparities includes a diverse group of Black women across various socioeconomic backgrounds. Many Black women face economic disadvantages that limit their access to quality healthcare. Economic instability often correlates with inadequate prenatal care and higher stress levels during pregnancy. Structural barriers such as lack of insurance, transportation issues, and geographic location can impede access to necessary medical services. Black women are more likely to be uninsured or underinsured compared to their white counterparts. The legacy of racism in healthcare has led to mistrust among Black communities towards medical institutions. Historical abuses, such as non-consensual medical experimentation on Black individuals, have fostered skepticism about the healthcare system's intentions and efficacy. These factors collectively contribute to poorer health outcomes for Black women during pregnancy and childbirth.

The legal landscape surrounding racial discrimination in healthcare has seen various lawsuits aimed at addressing discriminatory practices. Lawsuits have been filed against hospitals for failing to provide adequate care based on race. For example, cases have emerged where Black patients were denied timely treatments or faced longer wait times compared to white patients presenting similar symptoms. Some cases have resulted in settlements that mandate changes in hospital policies or increased training for staff on implicit bias and cultural competence. However, many cases highlight ongoing challenges in holding institutions accountable for systemic discrimination.

George Floyd

The protests that erupted following George Floyd's death on May 25th 2020, marked a significant moment in the ongoing struggle against systemic racism and police violence in the United States. George Floyd, a 46 year old black man, died after former Minneapolis police officer Derek Chauvin knelt on his neck for nearly nine minutes during an arrest for allegedly using a counterfeit $20 bill. The incident was captured on video by bystanders and quickly went viral, sparking outrage across the nation and around the world. The immediate aftermath saw widespread protests under the banner of the Black Lives Matter movement, demanding justice for Floyd and an end to police brutality. These demonstrations were not isolated to Minneapolis; they spread to cities across the country, with millions participating in calls for systemic change. The protests highlighted long standing issues of racial inequality and police violence, particularly against Black individuals, reigniting discussions about law enforcement practices and accountability.

As the protests unfolded, numerous reports emerged documenting instances of police violence against peaceful protesters. In cities like Portland, Oregon, and Minneapolis, law enforcement agencies deployed tear gas and rubber bullets against protesters. Reports indicated that these measures were often used indiscriminately, affecting not only demonstrators but also bystanders and journalists. A report from the

American Civil Liberties Union (ACLU) noted that tear gas was used in violation of international law governing the use of chemical agents in crowd control. In several instances, police officers were recorded violently arresting protesters. For example, in New York City, videos showed officers aggressively pushing protesters to the ground and using batons to disperse crowds. A significant incident involved officers driving into a crowd of protesters in Brooklyn, which raised alarms about the use of excessive force during peaceful demonstrations. The National Guard was deployed in multiple states to assist local law enforcement in managing protests. This militarization of police responses drew criticism from civil rights advocates who argued that it exacerbated tensions rather than promoting peace. These incidents fueled further outrage and calls for accountability from both local communities and national organizations advocating for civil rights.

One prominent case involved the City of Minneapolis, which faced multiple lawsuits related to its handling of protests following Floyd's death. The city ultimately agreed to a $27 million settlement with Floyd's family, one of the largest settlements in a police misconduct case in U.S. history. Plaintiffs often cite Section 1983 of the Civil Rights Act when suing police officers for constitutional violations. This statute allows individuals to seek redress for violations of their civil rights under color of state law, including excessive force claims. However, legal experts note that achieving justice through these lawsuits is challenging due to qualified immunity protections that shield officers from liability unless a clear constitutional violation can be demonstrated.

Evangelical Organizations In Discrimination Practices

Discrimination against Muslim Americans has become a pressing issue in contemporary society, marked by increased hostility and bias against individuals of the Islamic faith. This discrimination manifests in various forms, including social exclusion, workplace discrimination, and targeted violence. The relevance of this issue is underscored by a historical context that reveals a pattern of discrimination against immigrant populations in the United States, particularly those from Muslim majority countries.

Historically, immigrant populations in the U.S. have faced discrimination based on their nationality and religion. Following significant geopolitical events, such as the 9/11 attacks and subsequent military actions in predominantly Muslim countries, anti-Muslim sentiment surged. This context laid the groundwork for systemic discrimination that persists today.

Evangelical organizations have played a notable role in shaping public perceptions and policies regarding Muslim immigrants. Their involvement often stems from a combination of national security concerns and religious beliefs that view Islam as incompatible with American values.

Many Evangelical groups have framed their opposition to Muslim immigration within the context of national security. They argue that the influx of

Muslim immigrants poses a threat to American safety, often citing terrorism as a justification for their stance. This narrative has been reinforced by political rhetoric that emphasizes fear and suspicion towards Muslims. Some Evangelical organizations promote a worldview that sees Christianity as the only true faith, leading to a perception of Islam as a rival ideology. This perspective fuels discriminatory attitudes and practices, as these organizations may actively work to undermine the presence and influence of Muslim communities in the U.S.

The Family Research Council (FRC) has been vocal in its opposition to Muslim immigration, often promoting legislation that restricts entry for individuals from Muslim majority countries. The FRC has also disseminated literature that portrays Islam as inherently violent and incompatible with Western values. ACT for America was founded by Brigitte Gabriel, ACT for America is known for its anti-Muslim rhetoric and activism. The organization has organized rallies and campaigns aimed at raising awareness about what it describes as "Islamic extremism," often conflating all Muslims with extremists. Their initiatives have included lobbying for stricter immigration policies targeting Muslims. Some Evangelical groups have supported local policies that discriminate against Muslims, such as zoning laws that hinder the construction of mosques or Islamic centers. These actions reflect broader attempts to marginalize Muslim communities within predominantly Christian neighborhoods.

Discrimination fosters an environment of fear and alienation within Muslim communities. Many individuals report feeling unsafe or unwelcome in public spaces due to their religious identity. The psychological toll of discrimination can lead to anxiety, depression, and a sense of isolation among affected individuals. Community leaders emphasize the importance of mental health resources to support those grappling with these challenges. Discrimination can hinder economic opportunities for Muslim Americans, leading to unemployment or underemployment due to biases in hiring practices or workplace environments.

Refugees In Greece

Greece has been a significant entry point for refugees and migrants, particularly since the onset of the Syrian civil war in 2011. The country has faced an unprecedented influx of individuals seeking asylum, with many arriving via perilous sea routes from Turkey. As of 2021, it was estimated that over 100,000 refugees and migrants were living in Greece, with approximately 30,000 residing in camps on the islands and mainland. Human Rights Watch reported that conditions in these camps are often dire, characterized by overcrowding, inadequate sanitation, and limited access to healthcare and legal assistance. The ongoing economic crisis in Greece has further strained resources, complicating the situation for both local populations and refugees. Many refugees face bureaucratic hurdles that delay their asylum processes, leaving them in limbo for extended periods. This precarious situation has led to increased vulnerability among refugees, particularly women and children who are at higher risk of exploitation and abuse.

While many NGOs operate to support refugees in Greece, some Christian organizations have faced allegations of neglecting the needs of certain refugee groups. Reports indicate that aid distribution may favor specific religious communities over others, particularly Christians. For instance, organizations like Christian Aid Ministries have been criticized for prioritizing Christian refugees in their outreach programs. Their initiatives often focus on evangelism alongside humanitarian aid, which some argue can lead to the marginalization of Muslim refugees who do not share the same faith. Allegations suggest that resources such as food, shelter, and medical care may be disproportionately allocated to Christian individuals or families, leaving Muslim refugees without adequate support. Furthermore, instances have been documented where Christian organizations have engaged in proselytization efforts within refugee camps. This approach raises ethical concerns about the appropriateness of mixing humanitarian aid with religious conversion efforts, potentially alienating non-Christian refugees who may feel pressured or unwelcome.

The actions of certain NGOs can significantly impact the overall human rights situation for refugees in Greece. Discrimination based on religion not only violates principles of equality but also exacerbates the vulnerabilities faced by marginalized groups within the refugee population. When aid is distributed unevenly based on religious affiliation, it creates disparities in access to essential services such as food, healthcare, and shelter. This inequity can lead to increased suffering among those who are already vulnerable. Refugees who feel discriminated against due to their faith may experience heightened feelings of isolation and despair. The psychological toll can be profound, particularly for individuals who have already endured trauma from conflict or persecution. Favoritism towards specific religious groups can foster resentment among different communities within refugee camps. This tension can lead to conflicts that undermine social cohesion and safety.

George Washington And Slavery

George Washington, the first President of the United States and a key figure in the American Revolutionary War, is often celebrated as a founding father of American democracy. His leadership helped shape the nation, but his legacy is complicated by his status as a major slaveholder. Washington's relationship with slavery reflects the broader contradictions of American society during his lifetime, marked by ideals of liberty and the reality of human bondage.

Washington inherited his first slaves at the age of 11 from his father, who owned several slaves on their Virginia plantation. By the time he married Martha Custis in 1759, Washington had become a significant slaveholder himself. The context of slavery in 18th century Virginia was deeply entrenched; it was an economic system vital to the region's prosperity. Washington's Mount Vernon estate became a model of plantation agriculture, utilizing enslaved labor to produce tobacco, wheat, and other crops. At Mount Vernon, Washington operated five farms and owned over 500 enslaved individuals at various times throughout his life. The scale of enslaved labor was substantial, and Washington's management reflected both the economic imperatives of plantation life and the prevailing attitudes toward slavery among Virginia planters.

Enslaved individuals at Mount Vernon performed various roles essential to the plantation's operations. Approximately three quarters worked in agricultural capacities, tending to crops and livestock, while others served in domestic roles within the mansion. These domestic servants prepared meals, cleaned, and cared for Washington's family. The living conditions for enslaved people at Mount Vernon were harsh. Although Washington provided basic necessities such as food and shelter, these provisions were often inadequate. Reports indicate that some enslaved individuals lacked proper clothing and sufficient food. For instance, during winter months, children sometimes went without adequate clothing. Additionally, Washington's management style was strict; he expected hard work from his enslaved laborers and employed overseers to enforce discipline.

Washington's political actions during his lifetime also intersected with the institution of slavery. In 1787, he supported the Northwest Ordinance, which established governance for territories in the Northwest but also included provisions that allowed for slavery in certain areas. As president, Washington signed laws that both protected and curtailed slavery, reflecting the complex political landscape of early America.

Thomas Jefferson And Slavery

Thomas Jefferson, the third President of the United States and the principal author of the Declaration of Independence, is often heralded as a champion of liberty. However, his legacy is deeply intertwined with the institution of slavery. Born in 1743 in colonial Virginia, Jefferson inherited his first slaves from his father at a young age. Throughout his life, he would accumulate more than 450 enslaved individuals at his plantation, Monticello, and other properties. Jefferson's relationship with slavery began early, as he grew up on a plantation that relied on enslaved labor. By the time he became an adult, he had not only inherited slaves but also purchased more to sustain his agricultural endeavors. Monticello operated as a self-sufficient plantation where tobacco, wheat, and other crops were cultivated using enslaved labor. Jefferson's economic interests were thus closely tied to the continuation of slavery.

One of the most controversial aspects of Jefferson's life was his relationship with Sally Hemings, an enslaved woman who was also the half-sister of his late wife, Martha. Historians believe that Jefferson began a sexual relationship with Hemings when she was just 16 years old and he was 44. This relationship resulted in several children; six in total, four of whom survived to adulthood.

The implications of this relationship are profound. It raises questions about consent and power dynamics inherent in the master-slave relationship. Hemings' status as an enslaved person meant that she had no legal rights or autonomy; thus, any romantic involvement with Jefferson was inherently coercive. After Jefferson's death, it was revealed that he had freed two of their children, while others were allowed to escape without pursuit. This complex familial bond further complicates Jefferson's legacy as it highlights both his personal failings and the broader societal issues surrounding race and slavery.

Jefferson's political actions regarding slavery are marked by contradictions. Although he publicly condemned slavery as a "moral depravity," he also profited from it throughout his life. In 1808, during his presidency, Jefferson signed legislation that abolished the international slave trade, a significant step that reflected his long standing opposition to the importation of enslaved people. However, this action did not extend to ending slavery itself within the United States. Jefferson advocated for gradual emancipation but faced considerable challenges in implementing such policies. He believed that immediate emancipation would lead to social chaos and violence between freed blacks and white Americans. Instead, he proposed a plan for gradual emancipation coupled with colonization; resettling freed African Americans outside the United States. This paternalistic view reflected both his fears about racial integration and his belief in white superiority.

The legacy of Thomas Jefferson is fraught with contradictions. He is celebrated for articulating ideals of freedom and equality yet lived as a slave owner for most of his life. While he expressed opposition to the expansion of slavery into new territories fearing it would threaten the Union, he simultaneously maintained and expanded his own slaveholding practices at Monticello.

Jefferson's writings reveal an internal conflict; he recognized slavery as a profound moral failing yet felt unable to extricate himself from it due to economic reliance and societal norms. His famous declaration that "all men are created equal" stands in stark contrast to his actions as a slaveholder. This contradiction has led historians to debate whether Jefferson can be seen as an early advocate for abolition or merely a product of his time who failed to act on his principles.

James Madison And Slavery

James Madison, the fourth President of the United States and a key architect of the Constitution, is often celebrated for his contributions to American democracy and governance. However, his legacy is complicated by his relationship with slavery. Born in Virginia in 1751, Madison inherited a plantation and a significant number of enslaved individuals, which shaped both his personal life and political career. James Madison inherited over 100 enslaved individuals from his father, who owned Montpelier, a plantation in Virginia. Throughout his life, Madison would own almost 300 slaves, relying on their labor for agricultural production and household tasks. At Montpelier, enslaved people worked in various capacities, including farming tobacco, wheat, and other crops essential to the plantation's economy. The labor contributions of these individuals were crucial to Madison's financial success and social standing.

Despite acknowledging the moral implications of slavery, Madison's economic interests kept him tied to the institution. He did not free any of his slaves during his lifetime or in his will. Instead, he left them to his wife, Dolley Madison, with instructions that they should not be sold without their consent. However, this provision was not legally binding, and Dolley ultimately sold many of the enslaved individuals to pay off debts after Madison's death.

Madison's decision not to free his slaves can be attributed to a combination of societal pressures and personal circumstances. As a prominent figure in Virginia society, he was deeply entrenched in the slaveholding culture that dominated the Southern economy. The fear of economic instability and social upheaval played a significant role in his reluctance to emancipate his slaves. Madison believed that immediate emancipation would lead to chaos and conflict between freed blacks and white society. He expressed concerns about the ability of freed individuals to integrate into a society that held deep seated prejudices against them. His paternalistic views reflected a common sentiment among many slaveholders who saw themselves as guardians of their enslaved populations.

While Madison was a slave owner, he also opposed the international slave trade. He recognized it as morally reprehensible and detrimental to the nation's reputation. In 1808, he signed legislation that abolished the importation of enslaved individuals into the United States. This decision was influenced by growing abolitionist sentiments in the North and concerns about maintaining national unity. Madison's opposition stemmed from both ethical considerations and practical concerns about the stability of the republic he helped establish. He feared that an influx of enslaved individuals could exacerbate tensions between free and slave states, undermining the delicate balance necessary for political cohesion.

Despite his opposition to the international slave trade, Madison resisted efforts aimed at limiting the domestic expansion of slavery. He believed that as new territories were acquired through westward expansion, they should be open to slavery. During events such as the Missouri Crisis (1819-1821), Madison supported policies that allowed for the extension of slavery into new states. Madison's stance reflected a broader Southern interest in maintaining slavery as an integral part of American society. He feared that restricting slavery would threaten Southern economic interests and lead to increased sectional tensions. His actions during this period demonstrated a commitment to preserving slaveholding interests despite acknowledging the moral complexities surrounding slavery.

One of Madison's most significant contributions to American politics was his role in formulating the Three Fifths Compromise during the Constitutional Convention of 1787. This compromise allowed Southern states to count three fifths of their enslaved population for purposes of representation in Congress while also addressing taxation issues. Madison argued that this compromise was necessary for ensuring Southern participation in the new government framework. By counting enslaved individuals as partial persons for representation, slaveholding states gained greater political power while simultaneously reinforcing the notion that enslaved people were property rather than full citizens. This compromise had lasting implications for American politics and contributed to the systemic inequalities embedded within the Constitution.

James Monroe And Slavery

James Monroe, the fifth President of the United States, served from 1817 to 1825. Born on April 28th 1758, in Westmoreland County, Virginia, Monroe was a prominent figure in early American history. He played a crucial role in the founding of the nation, serving as a soldier in the Revolutionary War and later as a diplomat, governor, and cabinet member. Monroe is perhaps best known for the Monroe Doctrine, a cornerstone of American foreign policy. However, his legacy is also deeply intertwined with the institution of slavery, which shaped both his personal life and political decisions.

Throughout his adult life, James Monroe owned numerous slaves, primarily at his plantation, Highland, located in Virginia. While exact records vary, it is estimated that he owned over 100 slaves at various points during his life. These enslaved individuals were integral to the operation of his plantation, contributing labor for agricultural production and household tasks. At Highland, slaves worked in the fields cultivating tobacco and other crops essential to the plantation's economy. The conditions for these enslaved individuals were typical of the time; they faced long hours of labor under harsh supervision with limited provisions for their well-being. While Monroe did provide some basic necessities for his slaves such as food and shelter, their treatment reflected the broader societal norms of slavery during that era.

Later in life, Monroe made the decision to free only one slave, named Billy. This act occurred in 1820, shortly before his death in 1831. The significance of this decision is multifaceted; it highlights both Monroe's complex relationship with slavery and the societal pressures surrounding emancipation at the time. Monroe's decision to free Billy may have been motivated by personal feelings or a recognition of changing attitudes toward slavery. However, it also reflects a broader reluctance among slaveholders to emancipate their slaves fully. Many slaveholders feared that immediate emancipation would lead to social upheaval and violence. In freeing only one slave, Monroe maintained his status as a slave owner while also acknowledging the moral implications of slavery.

Monroe's political career was marked by significant actions regarding slavery. He supported the Missouri Compromise of 1820, which allowed Missouri to enter the Union as a slave state while Maine entered as a free state. This compromise aimed to maintain a balance between slave and free states in Congress but also highlighted the growing sectional tensions over slavery. Monroe's advocacy for colonization efforts aimed at sending freed slaves to Liberia is another critical aspect of his political actions regarding slavery. He was a member of the American Colonization Society, which promoted this initiative as a solution to what they perceived as the "problem" of free blacks in America. The rationale behind this movement included fears about racial integration and social stability. While some viewed colonization as an opportunity for freed slaves to establish their own communities, it ultimately reflected an unwillingness to accept African Americans as equal members of society within the United States.

Andrew Jackson And Slavery

Andrew Jackson, the seventh President of the United States, served from 1829 to 1837 and is often regarded as a pivotal figure in American history. Known for his populist approach and strong leadership style, Jackson's presidency marked significant developments in the nation, including the expansion of democracy and the controversial policies regarding Native American removal. However, his legacy is also deeply intertwined with the institution of slavery, as he was a prominent slave owner whose actions both reflected and reinforced pro-slavery sentiments in America. Andrew Jackson owned approximately 200 slaves throughout his adult life, primarily at his Tennessee plantation known as The Hermitage. He acquired most of these enslaved individuals through purchase and inheritance, managing them as part of his agricultural operations. The slaves at The Hermitage played crucial roles in both household duties and agricultural labor, working the fields to cultivate cotton, corn, and other crops essential to Jackson's wealth.

Jackson's management style reflected the paternalistic attitudes common among slave owners of his time. He sought to balance authority with a semblance of care for his enslaved workers. For instance, he expressed concern over their treatment by overseers and insisted on humane treatment to ensure productivity. However, this concern was often overshadowed by his financial interests; healthy and well-treated slaves were more likely to work efficiently and less likely to escape or rebel.

When Jackson became president, he brought several enslaved individuals from The Hermitage to serve in the White House. The 1830 census recorded 14 enslaved people living in Jackson's household, performing various domestic tasks such as cooking, cleaning, and serving guests. Their presence in the White House was indicative of the accepted norms of the time regarding slavery. The treatment of these enslaved individuals varied; while Jackson maintained a façade of paternalism, their status as property meant they had no rights or autonomy. Public perception of slavery during Jackson's presidency was complex; many Americans accepted it as a norm, yet there was growing opposition from abolitionists who criticized the institution as morally indefensible. Jackson's administration did not address these criticisms directly, reflecting a broader societal reluctance to confront the realities of slavery.

Jackson faced significant criticism for his involvement in the slave trade and his lack of support for anti-slavery movements. He was known to have participated in buying and selling slaves throughout his life, contributing to the expansion of slaveholding interests in America. His presidency coincided with growing abolitionist sentiments; however, he remained steadfastly opposed to these movements.

Jackson's actions often reinforced pro-slavery policies. For instance, he supported measures that expanded slaveholding interests during his time in office. His administration actively sought to maintain the balance between free and slave states while promoting the interests of Southern slaveholders. This included opposing any significant federal action that might threaten slavery's expansion into new territories.

Jackson's presidency had a profound impact on pro-slavery sentiments in America. His strong advocacy for states' rights and expansionism aligned with Southern interests that sought to entrench slavery further into American society. By supporting policies that favored slaveholding states such as the Missouri Compromise. Jackson helped solidify a political landscape where slavery was increasingly viewed as integral to Southern identity. The sectional tensions that arose during Jackson's presidency set the stage for future conflicts over slavery. His administration's reluctance to confront abolitionist movements or limit slavery's expansion contributed to an environment where pro-slavery ideologies flourished. This laid the groundwork for escalating tensions between North and South that would eventually culminate in the Civil War.

Martin Van Buren And Slavery

Martin Van Buren, the eighth President of the United States, served from 1837 to 1841 during a tumultuous period in American history. Born on December 5th 1782, in Kinderhook, New York, Van Buren was raised in a household where slavery was a part of the social fabric. His father owned several slaves, and this early exposure influenced his political career. Van Buren studied law and quickly ascended through the ranks of the Democratic Party, eventually becoming a key ally of President Andrew Jackson. His political career included roles as a New York state senator, governor, U.S. senator, Secretary of State, and Vice President before he was elected president. Van Buren's presidency coincided with rising tensions over slavery and its expansion into new territories. His administration faced significant challenges, including economic downturns and sectional strife that would eventually lead to the Civil War.

Throughout his life, Martin Van Buren owned one enslaved person named Tom. The circumstances surrounding Tom's escape are notable; he managed to flee from Van Buren's control, highlighting the complexities of slavery even among those who might have been perceived as benevolent slave owners. Van Buren's ownership of Tom occurred during a time when New York had begun to shift towards gradual emancipation, culminating in the abolition of slavery in the state by 1827. While serving as president, Van Buren did not own slaves. However, his previous involvement with slavery as a landowner in New York remained a part of his legacy. He inherited the societal norms of his upbringing, which included an acceptance of slavery as a legal institution.

Van Buren's political career unfolded against a backdrop of significant changes regarding slavery in America. As he rose through political ranks in New York, he witnessed the gradual emancipation law passed in 1799 that stipulated children born to enslaved mothers after July 4th would be freed by July 4th 1827. This law reflected a growing awareness of the moral implications of slavery among Northern politicians. During Van Buren's presidency, tensions between the North and South escalated dramatically. The Missouri Compromise of 1820 had temporarily settled disputes over the expansion of slavery into new territories but left underlying issues unresolved. The political climate was charged with debates over states' rights and federal authority concerning slavery.

Van Buren's presidency is characterized by a notably neutral stance on slavery. He sought to maintain peace between pro-slavery and anti-slavery factions but often did so at the expense of taking decisive action against slavery itself. For instance, while he acknowledged that slavery was a "moral evil," he refrained from supporting any significant legislative measures aimed at abolishing or limiting it.

One notable event during his presidency was his involvement in the Amistad case. In this incident, enslaved Africans aboard a Spanish ship revolted and took control of the vessel. After being captured off the coast of Long Island, they were brought to trial in the United States. Van Buren's administration sought to return the Africans to Spain to appease diplomatic relations but faced fierce opposition from abolitionists who argued for their freedom. Ultimately, the Supreme Court ruled in favor of the Africans shortly after Van Buren left office, marking a significant moment for the abolitionist movement.

Van Buren also supported congressional gag rules that prohibited discussions about anti-slavery petitions in Congress, further illustrating his reluctance to confront the issue directly.

Van Buren's presidency reinforced pro-slavery sentiments within American politics. His attempts to appease Southern interests while maintaining Northern support positioned him as a transitional figure between earlier slaveholding presidents and those who actively opposed slavery. By avoiding strong anti-slavery stances or actions during his administration, he contributed to an environment where pro-slavery ideologies could flourish. His alignment with Southern Democrats earned him criticism from abolitionists and those advocating for civil rights for African Americans. The tensions that arose during his presidency set the stage for future conflicts over slavery that would eventually culminate in civil war.

William Henry Harrison And Slavery

William Henry Harrison, the ninth President of the United States, was born on February 9th 1773, in Charles City County, Virginia. He came from a prominent family; his father, Benjamin Harrison V, was a signer of the Declaration of Independence and a governor of Virginia. Harrison's upbringing in a slaveholding family shaped his views on slavery and influenced his political career. Harrison inherited several slaves from his family and later acquired more throughout his life. By the time he became a landowner in the Northwest Territory, he was involved in the complex dynamics of slavery and land ownership. His estate included a plantation where enslaved individuals worked in agricultural production, reflecting the economic realities of his time.

Harrison served as the governor of the Indiana Territory from 1800 to 1812. During his tenure, he sought to promote settlement and economic development in the region. One of his controversial goals was to legalize slavery in Indiana. At that time, the Northwest Ordinance of 1787 prohibited slavery in the Northwest Territory, which included Indiana. Harrison lobbied Congress to temporarily suspend this prohibition for ten years to encourage settlement and make the territory economically viable. He believed that allowing slavery would attract more settlers from slaveholding states. However, his proposal faced fierce opposition from abolitionists and anti-slavery advocates within Indiana and Congress. The political climate in Indiana was shifting; as more settlers arrived from free states, anti-slavery sentiments grew stronger.

Ultimately, Harrison's attempts to legalize slavery failed. In 1807, the territorial legislature enacted laws that allowed for indentured servitude but did not permit outright slavery. This legislative outcome reflected the growing influence of anti-slavery factions in Indiana and marked a significant defeat for Harrison's pro-slavery agenda.

William Henry Harrison's presidency was notably brief; he served only 31 days before dying of pneumonia in April 1841. His short term did not allow for significant legislation regarding slavery or any major policy initiatives. However, during his campaign for presidency, he maintained a neutral stance on slavery, reflecting the divided sentiments of the nation at that time. While in office, Harrison did not take any decisive actions regarding slavery. His lack of engagement with the issue can be interpreted as an attempt to avoid alienating either pro-slavery or anti-slavery constituents during a period marked by increasing sectional tensions. The broader implications of his presidency on national conversations about slavery were limited due to its brevity; however, it occurred during a critical juncture when debates over slavery were intensifying.

Harrison's legacy is complicated by his relationship with slavery and the national conflict surrounding it.

While he is often remembered for his military achievements and as a figure who represented frontier expansionism, his pro-slavery inclinations cannot be overlooked. As a former governor who attempted to legalize slavery in Indiana, Harrison's actions contributed to the entrenchment of pro-slavery sentiments in American politics.

John Tyler And Slavery

John Tyler, the 10th President of the United States, served from 1841 to 1845, following the death of William Henry Harrison. His presidency is often noted for its challenges, including a lack of party support and significant political isolation. Tyler was a member of the Whig Party but frequently clashed with its leaders, particularly over issues related to states' rights and slavery. His historical significance lies not only in his presidency but also in his role as a Southern leader during a time of increasing sectional conflict, which ultimately contributed to the Civil War.

Tyler's relationship with slavery was deeply rooted in his family background. Born into a prominent Virginia family in 1790, he inherited enslaved individuals from his father, who was a wealthy farmer. By the time Tyler was an adult, he owned approximately 24 slaves at his Woodburn plantation, having inherited 13 from his father and acquired more through purchases. Over his lifetime, estimates suggest that Tyler owned between at least several hundred slaves, many of whom worked on his plantations and in domestic roles at the White House during his presidency.

The enslaved individuals on Tyler's plantations performed various tasks, from agricultural labor to household duties. This reliance on enslaved labor was typical for Southern planters, who viewed slavery as integral to their economic success. Tyler's ownership and management of slaves reflected the broader societal norms of his time, where slavery was often justified as a necessary institution for the Southern economy.

Tyler's views on slavery were complex and often contradictory. While he expressed personal disdain for the institution considering it a "necessary evil", his political actions consistently supported its continuation and expansion. He believed that slavery should be allowed anywhere in the United States and opposed any federal attempts to regulate or restrict it. In private correspondence, Tyler articulated concerns about the moral implications of slavery but simultaneously defended it politically. For instance, he once remarked that "the institution of slavery is a necessary evil," indicating a recognition of its moral complexities while still advocating for its preservation. This duality highlights the tension many Southern leaders faced; acknowledging the moral issues surrounding slavery while actively supporting its existence for economic and political reasons.

One of Tyler's most significant political actions related to slavery was his advocacy for the annexation of Texas. Texas had declared independence from Mexico in 1836 and sought to join the United States as a slave state. Tyler believed that annexing Texas would prevent British influence in North America and bolster the power of slaveholding states within the Union. The annexation was controversial and tied directly to the expansion of slavery into new territories, which heightened tensions between free and slave states. Tyler's push for annexation was seen as an attempt to secure more political power for the South at a time when sectional divisions were intensifying.

During his presidency, Tyler's legislative actions reflected his pro-slavery stance. He appointed several Southern slaveholders to key positions within his administration and supported policies that favored the expansion of slavery into new territories. For example, he opposed the Missouri Compromise of 1820, which aimed to limit the spread of slavery into new states formed from western territories. Tyler argued that such restrictions were unconstitutional and detrimental to Southern interests. Despite these positions, Tyler faced significant challenges in advancing pro-slavery legislation due to opposition from both Whigs and Democrats who were increasingly divided over slavery issues. His presidency is characterized by a lack of substantial legislative achievements regarding slavery, largely due to his contentious relationships with Congress.

Tyler's actions significantly contributed to the growing sectional divide in the United States leading up to the Civil War. By advocating for policies that favored slave states and opposing measures designed to limit slavery's expansion, he exacerbated tensions between Northern abolitionists and Southern slaveholders. His support for Texas annexation is particularly notable; it not only increased the number of slave states but also ignited fierce debates about the future of slavery in American politics. As sectional conflicts intensified during his presidency, Tyler's inability to bridge divides or propose effective compromises further alienated him from both major political parties. His legacy became intertwined with these growing tensions, marking him as a figure emblematic of Southern resistance against Northern abolitionist sentiments.

James K. Polk And Slavery

James K. Polk served as the 11th President of the United States from 1845 to 1849. His presidency is often noted for its significant territorial expansion, particularly through the Mexican-American War, which resulted in the acquisition of vast lands that would later become states in the Union. During Polk's time, slavery was a deeply entrenched institution in American society, particularly in the Southern states, where it was integral to the economy and social structure. The political climate was charged with debates over the expansion of slavery into new territories, setting the stage for future conflicts that would culminate in the Civil War.

Polk's relationship with slavery was personal as well as political. He owned approximately 30 slaves at his Mississippi plantation, which he managed from a distance while serving in public office. His slaves were primarily involved in cotton production, a labor intensive crop that required substantial manpower. Polk acquired many of these enslaved individuals through inheritance and purchase; his family had a long history of slave ownership, and he continued this legacy by purchasing additional slaves to expand his workforce. By the time of his death in 1849, Polk's holdings had increased to over 50 slaves. His management style reflected the typical practices of Southern planters; he relied on overseers to maintain productivity and discipline on his plantation. While he occasionally intervened on behalf of enslaved individuals who faced harsh treatment, these actions were often motivated by economic considerations rather than genuine concern for their well-being.

Polk's presidency was marked by aggressive territorial expansion, particularly following the Mexican-American War (1846-1848). He believed that expanding U.S. territory was essential for national growth and prosperity, but this expansion also raised critical questions about the status of slavery in newly acquired lands. Polk supported the idea that slavery should be allowed in these territories, which intensified national debates over whether new states would enter the Union as free or slave states. The political climate during this period was fraught with tension. The Wilmot Proviso, introduced by Congressman David Wilmot in 1846, sought to ban slavery in any territory acquired from Mexico. Although it passed in the House of Representatives, it failed in the Senate, highlighting the deep divisions within Congress along sectional lines. Polk's support for allowing slavery's expansion into new territories exacerbated tensions between Northern and Southern states and contributed to a growing sectional divide.

The debates surrounding slavery during Polk's presidency ultimately laid the groundwork for the Compromise of 1850. This series of legislative measures aimed to address the contentious issue of slavery's expansion into new territories following California's admission as a free state. The Compromise sought to balance interests between slaveholding and free states but also revealed deep seated divisions within both major political parties. California's admission as a free state was particularly significant because it disrupted the balance of power between free and slave states in Congress. The Compromise included provisions such as popular sovereignty for other territories acquired from Mexico, allowing settlers to decide whether to permit slavery. However, these measures did little to quell the growing tensions over slavery and only postponed inevitable conflicts.

Polk's presidency and his staunch support for slavery set a precedent that intensified national debates about this institution. His actions during his term contributed significantly to sectional tensions that would lead directly to future conflicts, including John Brown's raid on Harpers Ferry and ultimately the Civil War. Polk's policies were seen as an attempt to secure Southern dominance in national politics through territorial expansion that favored slaveholding interests. This approach alienated many Northern Democrats and Whigs who opposed extending slavery into new territories, leading to fractures within political parties that would later manifest in new movements like the Republican Party.

Zachary Taylor

Zachary Taylor was born on November 24th 1784, near Barboursville, Virginia, into a prominent family of plantation owners. His father, Richard Taylor, was a veteran of the Revolutionary War and owned a substantial amount of land in Kentucky and Virginia. The family moved to Louisville, Kentucky, where Taylor spent his formative years on a tobacco plantation. He received a basic education but was primarily trained in military tactics and agriculture. Taylor's military career began in 1808 when he was commissioned as a first lieutenant in the U.S. Army. Over the next four decades, he rose through the ranks, earning national acclaim for his leadership during the Mexican-American War. His victories at battles such as Palo Alto and Buena Vista established him as a national hero, which ultimately paved the way for his election as the 12th President of the United States in 1848. Taylor's presidency lasted only 16 months until his death on July 9th 1850, from an illness that struck him suddenly.

During his lifetime, Zachary Taylor owned plantations in both Louisiana and Mississippi. His main plantation was located in Baton Rouge, Louisiana, known as Cypress Grove. At this plantation, Taylor managed approximately 100 enslaved individuals, who were primarily engaged in the labor intensive production of cotton and other crops. The operation relied heavily on enslaved labor to sustain its profitability. Taylor's wealth and status were largely derived from his plantation holdings and slave labor. He inherited some enslaved people from his family and acquired more through purchase over time. This ownership was not uncommon for Southern gentlemen of his era, who viewed slavery as an integral part of their economic success.

During his presidency, Taylor brought several enslaved individuals with him to Washington D.C., where they served as domestic staff in the White House. This practice was common among many Southern presidents who owned slaves, reflecting the social norms of the time. The presence of enslaved people in the Executive Mansion highlighted the contradictions inherent in American democracy where leaders espoused liberty while simultaneously benefiting from slavery. The implications of this action were significant. By bringing enslaved individuals into a federal space, Taylor contributed to the ongoing debate about slavery's legitimacy within the nation's capital. His administration faced scrutiny from abolitionists and free-soil advocates who opposed slavery's expansion into new territories and questioned its morality.

Zachary Taylor's political stance on slavery was complex and often contradictory. Although he was a slave owner himself, he opposed the extension of slavery into newly acquired territories from Mexico following the Mexican-American War. This position put him at odds with many Southern leaders who sought to expand slaveholding interests into these new lands. Taylor believed that California and New

Mexico should be admitted as free states without going through a territorial phase that would allow for slavery's expansion. His opposition to extending slavery angered many Southern politicians who felt betrayed by a fellow slaveholder who did not support their interests. This stance created tension with Congress and contributed to divisions within the Whig Party.

One of the most significant issues during Taylor's presidency was California's admission as a free state following its rapid population growth due to the Gold Rush in 1849. Taylor supported California's application for statehood without allowing it to become a territory first; a move designed to bypass potential conflicts over whether it would permit slavery. This decision had far reaching implications for the political landscape of the time. The admission of California as a free state disrupted the delicate balance between free and slave states in Congress, leading to heightened tensions between Northern and Southern factions.

Taylor's opposition to slavery's expansion significantly impacted the political climate leading up to the Civil War. His presidency coincided with increasing sectional tensions over slavery, particularly concerning newly acquired territories from Mexico. By advocating for free state status for California and opposing slavery's spread, Taylor intensified debates about states' rights versus federal authority regarding slavery. His actions contributed to growing discontent among Southern leaders who felt that their interests were being sidelined by Northern politicians. This division ultimately fueled movements toward secession among Southern states and laid groundwork for future conflicts that would culminate in the Civil War.

Violent Pushbacks In Croatia (2019-2021)

The period from 2019 to 2021 saw a significant increase in migration attempts along the Balkan route, with Croatia becoming a key transit point for migrants and refugees seeking entry into the European Union. This influx led to heightened border control measures, resulting in numerous reports of violent pushbacks at the Croatia-Bosnia border. Pushbacks, in this context, refer to the practice of forcibly returning migrants and asylum seekers across a border without due process or consideration of their individual circumstances, often involving violence and human rights violations.

Between 2019 and 2021, multiple incidents of violent pushbacks were reported along the Croatia-Bosnia border. The Danish Refugee Council (DRC) documented over 16,000 pushbacks from Croatia to Bosnia and Herzegovina during this period, with a sharp increase in violence observed from May 2020 onwards. One particularly brutal incident occurred in October 2020, when 16 Pakistani and Afghan migrants were allegedly beaten and robbed by Croatian police before being pushed back into Bosnia. The victims reported severe injuries, including broken arms and ribs. In another case in May 2021, a group of migrants, including women and children, were forcibly returned to Bosnia after attempting to cross into Croatia. They reported being beaten with batons, kicked, and having their belongings destroyed by Croatian border police. The methods employed by

Croatian border police during these pushbacks were characterized by extreme brutality; beatings with batons, fists, and feet, confiscation of money, phones, and other valuables, breaking or burning migrants' possessions, pushing migrants back across the border without due process and intimidation tactics to instill fear sometimes using dogs.

The DRC reported that 60% of pushback cases involved physical abuse and excessive use of force. In some instances, migrants were stripped of their clothing and shoes before being forced to walk back across the border in freezing temperatures. Article 3 of the European Convention on Human Rights (ECHR) prohibits torture and inhuman or degrading treatment. Article 4 of Protocol No. 4 of the ECHR prohibits of collective expulsion of aliens.

The practice of pushbacks denies individuals the right to seek asylum and violates the principle of non-refoulement, which prohibits returning individuals to countries where they may face persecution or harm.

A study by Medecins Sans Frontieres (MSF) found that 70% of migrants treated in their clinics in Serbia reported experiencing violence during their journey, with a significant portion attributing this violence to encounters with border authorities. The Croatian government has consistently denied allegations of violent pushbacks, claiming that their border police operate within the law. However, mounting evidence and international pressure have led to some responses. In October 2021, the European

Commission called on Croatia to investigate the allegations and establish an independent border monitoring mechanism. The Croatian Interior Ministry announced internal investigations into some reported incidents, but critics argue these lack transparency and impartiality. The European Court of Human Rights has received several applications related to pushbacks in Croatia, potentially leading to future legal consequences for the state. Despite these measures, human rights organizations argue that accountability remains insufficient, with few concrete steps taken to prevent future violations or punish those responsible for past abuses.

Human Rights Violations In Greek Island Refugee Camps

The refugee crisis that began in 2015 saw a significant influx of asylum seekers arriving on Greek islands, leading to the establishment of overcrowded and often inhumane detention facilities. The refugee camps on Greek islands have been characterized by severe overcrowding and inadequate sanitation facilities. In 2020, the Moria camp on Lesbos, designed to house 3,000 people, held over 20,000 asylum seekers, creating dire living conditions. Refugees were forced to live in makeshift shelters, often without access to basic necessities such as clean water and proper waste management systems; insufficient toilet facilities, with reports of one toilet per 200 people in some camps, limited access to showers and hygiene products, overcrowded sleeping areas, with multiple families sharing small tents or containers and inadequate food distribution and lack of proper nutrition. These conditions violate basic human rights standards and pose significant health risks to the camp residents.

The conditions in Greek refugee camps violate several international and European legal standards; Article 3 of the European Convention on Human Rights (ECHR) prohibits inhuman or degrading treatment. The European Court of Human Rights has ruled that detention conditions can amount to a violation of Article 3 if they fail to meet basic standards of hygiene, space, and dignity.

The overcrowded and unsanitary conditions in Greek refugee camps have led to severe health consequences for detainees. Increased risk of infectious diseases due to poor sanitation and overcrowding. Malnutrition and related health issues due to inadequate food supply. Untreated chronic conditions due to limited access to healthcare services. High rates of depression, anxiety, and post-traumatic stress disorder (PTSD). Increased incidents of self-harm and suicidal ideation. Psychological distress exacerbated by prolonged uncertainty and poor living conditions. A study conducted by Medecins Sans Frontieres in 2020 found that 60% of new adult patients in their mental health clinic on Lesbos had considered suicide.

Certain groups within the refugee population face heightened risks due to the camp conditions specifically women, girls and children. Increased risk of sexual and gender based violence, lack of privacy and inadequate sanitation facilities, limited access to reproductive health services, disrupted education and developmental delays, exposure to violence and exploitation and psychological trauma impacting long term well-being. Individuals with pre-existing health conditions are also affected by inadequate medical care for chronic illnesses and increased risk of health deterioration due to poor living conditions.

A report by Human Rights Watch in 2020 documented cases of unaccompanied minors being detained with unrelated adults, exposing them to potential abuse and exploitation.

Human Rights Violations Related To The Denial of Rescue At Sea

The Mediterranean Sea has become a critical area for migrant crossings, with thousands attempting perilous journeys in search of safety and a better life. Between 2018 and 2023, numerous human rights violations have occurred related to the denial of rescue at sea, culminating in tragic incidents such as the Pylos shipwreck in June 2023. The period from 2018 to 2023 saw a series of harrowing incidents involving the denial of rescue operations in the Mediterranean. Multiple reports document instances where rescue ships operated by NGOs were denied entry into Italian ports. The Italian government implemented stringent measures against these vessels, often citing security concerns.

One of the most significant tragedies occurred when a boat carrying approximately 750 migrants capsized off the coast of Pylos, Greece. Despite distress calls made to authorities, no timely rescue was executed. Reports indicate that only about 104 individuals were rescued, while hundreds remain unaccounted for. Survivors recounted being left adrift for hours before any assistance arrived.

In August 2021 a boat carrying over 100 migrants was stranded for days without rescue despite being spotted by authorities. This incident highlighted a troubling pattern of delayed responses to distress calls.

These incidents reflect a broader trend of increasing hostility towards migrant rescues in the Mediterranean, often influenced by political pressures and anti-migrant sentiment. Under various administrations since 2018, Italy has adopted increasingly restrictive policies regarding maritime rescues. The government has often refused to allow NGO operated rescue ships to dock, citing legal and security concerns. This refusal has led to prolonged standoffs at sea, with ships carrying vulnerable individuals unable to disembark. Malta has similarly been criticized for its handling of maritime rescues. The country frequently claims that it lacks the capacity to assist all vessels in distress, leading to delays in rescue operations and increased risks for those stranded at sea. These patterns indicate a systemic refusal to engage in humanitarian rescues effectively, prioritizing political considerations over human lives.

Article 2 of the European Convention on Human Rights (ECHR) enshrines the right to life and obligates states to take appropriate measures to protect individuals from threats to their lives. The failure to conduct timely rescues directly contravenes this obligation. Under international maritime law, particularly the United Nations Convention on the Law of the Sea (UNCLOS) and the International Convention on Maritime Search and Rescue (SAR), states are required to assist vessels in distress without delay. The repeated failures to adhere to these laws during rescue operations represent serious violations that endanger lives at sea.

Hungary's Treatment of Asylum Seekers

Hungary's treatment of asylum seekers between 2015 and 2019 raised serious human rights concerns, particularly regarding the systematic denial of food to those held in transit zones along the country's southern border. This practice, implemented by the Hungarian government, violated fundamental human rights principles and contravened both EU asylum law and the European Convention on Human Rights (ECHR).

In 2015, at the height of the European migrant crisis, Hungary constructed a border fence and established transit zones to process asylum claims. These zones, located in Roszke and Tompa, became de facto detention centers where asylum seekers were held for extended periods. Between 2015 and 2019, the Hungarian government implemented a policy of denying food to adult asylum seekers in transit zones whose initial asylum applications had been rejected. This practice was particularly egregious given that these individuals were effectively detained and unable to leave to obtain food elsewhere.

Statistics from the Hungarian Helsinki Committee, a human rights organization, revealed at least 21 cases of food deprivation were documented between August 2018 and April 2019. Asylum seekers were denied food for up to 5 days at a time. In some cases, individuals lost up to 10 kg of body weight due to food deprivation.

One notable case involved an Afghan family with three children who were held in the Roszke transit zone. While the children were provided with food, their parents were denied sustenance for several days, leading to severe hunger and health deterioration. Another case involved a pregnant woman who was denied food for three days, putting both her health and that of her unborn child at risk.

The practice of denying food to asylum seekers clearly violated Article 3 of the ECHR, which prohibits inhuman or degrading treatment. The European Court of Human Rights (ECHR) ruled on multiple occasions that Hungary's actions constituted a breach of this fundamental right. Furthermore, this practice contravened EU asylum law, specifically the Reception Conditions Directive, which requires member states to ensure an adequate standard of living for asylum seekers, including access to sufficient food.

The denial of food often led to forced departures, as asylum seekers felt compelled to leave Hungary to avoid starvation. This practice effectively circumvented proper asylum procedures and potentially exposed individuals to further risks in other countries.

The Hungarian government attempted to justify its actions by claiming that rejected asylum seekers were free to leave the transit zones and return to Serbia. However, this argument was rejected by both the ECHR and human rights organizations, who pointed out that such departures could result in loss of asylum rights and potential refoulement.

International bodies, including the United Nations High Commissioner for Refugees (UNHCR) and the European Commission, strongly condemned Hungary's practices and called for immediate cessation of food deprivation.

The EU Relocation Scheme

The EU Relocation Scheme, initiated in 2015, aimed to address the influx of refugees and migrants arriving in Europe, particularly in response to the Syrian civil war and other crises. Its primary objective was to redistribute asylum seekers from frontline countries, such as Italy and Greece, to other EU member states in a bid to alleviate pressure on those nations and ensure a more equitable distribution of responsibilities among EU countries. However, this scheme has been criticized for its implementation, particularly regarding family separations that occurred during the relocation process.

Family unity is a fundamental human right recognized under international law, especially articulated in Article 8 of the European Convention on Human Rights (ECHR), which guarantees the right to respect for private and family life. The significance of maintaining family unity is paramount, as separations can lead to profound emotional and psychological distress for individuals and families, undermining their well-being and stability.

During the implementation of the EU Relocation Scheme from 2015 to 2018, numerous families experienced separation due to various procedural and logistical challenges. Lengthy processing times for asylum applications often resulted in family members being relocated to different countries before their claims were resolved. Variations in national policies regarding asylum seekers led to inconsistencies in how families were treated across EU member states. Poor communication between authorities and families regarding relocation decisions often left individuals unaware of their family members' whereabouts.

Several poignant case studies highlight the impact of these separations. The Al-Masri family; a Syrian family was separated when the father was relocated to Germany while the mother and children remained in Greece. The separation lasted over a year, causing significant emotional distress for both parents and children. The Ahmed Family; after fleeing from Iraq, the Ahmed family was split when one sibling was sent to France while the others were placed in Italy. The siblings faced immense psychological challenges due to their separation. These examples underscore the human cost associated with administrative processes that overlook the importance of family unity.

Article 8 ECHR emphasizes that everyone has the right to respect for their private and family life. This provision has been interpreted by the European Court of Human Rights (ECHR) as imposing a positive obligation on states to take necessary measures to protect family life. The actions taken under the EU Relocation Scheme have raised significant concerns regarding potential violations of this right. By facilitating family separations without adequate safeguards or consideration for familial ties, member states may have breached their obligations under Article 8. The lack of coherent policies that prioritize family unity further exacerbates this issue.

Human Rights Violations At The Polish-Belarusian Border

The Polish-Belarusian border crisis that unfolded between 2021 and 2023 has been marked by severe human rights violations, drawing international concern and criticism. The crisis began in mid-2021 when Belarus, under the leadership of Alexander Lukashenko, allegedly orchestrated an influx of migrants to its borders with EU countries, particularly Poland, Lithuania, and Latvia. This action was widely perceived as retaliation against EU sanctions imposed on Belarus following the disputed 2020 Belarusian presidential election and subsequent crackdown on opposition. Thousands of migrants, primarily from Middle Eastern and African countries, attempted to cross into Poland from Belarus. The Polish government responded by reinforcing its border security and implementing stringent measures to prevent unauthorized entry.

One of the most concerning aspects of the crisis has been the violent pushbacks conducted by Polish border guards. Numerous reports from human rights organizations and media outlets have documented instances of excessive force used against migrants attempting to cross the border. Use of water cannons and tear gas against groups of migrants, including women and children. Physical assaults on individuals caught crossing the border, resulting in injuries. Forceful deportations back to Belarus, often conducted at night and in remote areas. According to data from the Polish Border Guard, there were over 40,000 attempted border crossings in 2021 alone, with many individuals subjected to pushbacks.

Poland has been criticized for systematically denying access to proper asylum procedures for individuals at the border. This practice violates international refugee law and EU regulations, which require member states to allow individuals to apply for asylum and have their claims fairly assessed. The actions of Polish authorities at the border raise serious concerns regarding the violation of the non-refoulement principle. This principle, enshrined in international law and specifically in Article 3 of the European Convention on Human Rights (ECHR), prohibits states from returning individuals to countries where they may face persecution, torture, or inhuman treatment. By forcibly returning migrants to Belarus without proper assessment of their individual circumstances, Poland potentially exposes these individuals to further harm. Belarus has been criticized for its poor human rights record, and there are concerns that returned migrants may face abuse or be forced to attempt dangerous border crossings again.

The humanitarian situation at the border has been dire. Migrants have faced extreme conditions; exposure to harsh weather, with temperatures dropping well below freezing in winter months, lack of adequate shelter, food, and clean water and limited access to medical care, leading to deteriorating health conditions.

Tragically, there have been reports of deaths at the border. According to humanitarian organizations, at least 21 people died while attempting to cross from Belarus into Poland in 2021 alone. Causes of death included hypothermia and exhaustion.

The United Nations High Commissioner for Refugees (UNHCR) has repeatedly called on Poland to provide access to asylum procedures and to stop pushbacks. Human rights organizations such as Amnesty International and Human Rights Watch have documented violations and called for immediate action. The European Commission has urged Poland to allow EU border agency Frontex to operate at the border to ensure compliance with EU law.

Despite these calls, the Polish government has largely maintained its stance, arguing that its actions are necessary to protect national security and the integrity of the EU's external borders.

Inadequate Reception of Unaccompanied Minors

Unaccompanied minors are defined as children under the age of 18 who arrive in a country without the presence of a parent or legal guardian. Their protection is paramount under international law, particularly the UN Convention on the Rights of the Child, which mandates that states ensure the safety and well-being of all children, regardless of their status. The European refugee crisis from 2015 to 2023 saw a significant influx of unaccompanied minors into Europe, particularly through countries like Greece and Italy. Unaccompanied minors arriving in Greece and Italy have encountered numerous human rights violations, including inadequate shelter, lack of access to education, and exposure to violence and exploitation. According to Eurostat, over 92,000 unaccompanied minors applied for asylum in EU countries in 2015 alone, with Greece and Italy being primary entry points.

In Greece, many unaccompanied minors have been placed in overcrowded camps with insufficient facilities. Reports indicate that as of 2022, approximately 3,000 unaccompanied minors were living in inadequate conditions, often lacking basic necessities such as food, clean water, and medical care. In Italy, similar issues persist; many minors are housed in temporary shelters that do not meet child protection standards. National authorities bear the responsibility for the care and protection of unaccompanied minors under both EU regulations and the UN Convention on the Rights of the Child. However, both Greece and Italy have faced significant challenges in fulfilling these obligations.

The consequences of inadequate reception for unaccompanied minors are dire. Many minors face heightened risks of trafficking due to their vulnerable status. A report by Europol highlighted that unaccompanied minors are particularly susceptible to exploitation by criminal networks. Education is a fundamental right; however, many unaccompanied minors are unable to access schooling due to bureaucratic hurdles and language barriers. In Italy, only about 30% of unaccompanied minors were enrolled in school as of 2021. The psychological impact on these children can be profound. Studies indicate that many suffer from anxiety, depression, and PTSD due to their experiences during migration and inadequate reception conditions.

The legal framework protecting unaccompanied minors includes various EU laws such as the Dublin Regulation, which governs asylum procedures within member states, and the EU Reception Conditions Directive, which sets minimum standards for reception conditions. Despite these laws being in place, their implementation has been inconsistent across member states. In practice, many countries prioritize border control over compliance with human rights obligations. The inadequacies in Greece's and Italy's reception systems highlight significant gaps between legal standards and actual practices on the ground.

EU Financial Support for Refugee Accommodation

The refugee crisis in Europe has escalated significantly over the past decade, driven by conflicts, persecution, and socio-economic instability in various regions. The influx of refugees, particularly from Syria, Afghanistan, and more recently Ukraine, has put immense pressure on EU member states to provide adequate accommodation and support services. In 2024, Europe is projected to host approximately 24.9 million forcibly displaced individuals, highlighting the ongoing need for effective refugee management strategies. The European Union (EU) plays a crucial role in addressing these challenges through financial support mechanisms aimed at enhancing the accommodation and integration of refugees.

The EU employs several funding instruments to support member states in managing refugee accommodation. Asylum, Migration and Integration Fund (AMIF) with a budget of €9.88 billion for 2021-2027, AMIF aims to strengthen the common European asylum system and enhance solidarity among member states. It funds projects related to asylum procedures, integration measures, and infrastructure improvements for reception facilities. European Social Fund (ESF) supports social inclusion initiatives and can be utilized to improve housing conditions for vulnerable populations, including refugees. The ESF focuses on enhancing access to employment and education for migrants. Emergency Support Instrument (ESI) provides urgent financial assistance to member states facing sudden influxes of migrants. It has been used extensively in Greece and Italy to improve reception conditions and provide immediate support services. Allocation of these funds is typically done through national programs where member states propose projects that align with EU objectives. The EU then assesses these proposals and allocates funds accordingly.

Greece has been one of the primary recipients of EU funding due to its geographical position as a frontline state in the refugee crisis. Between 2014 and 2020, Greece received approximately €2.27 billion from AMIF alone. Key projects funded include; Harmonizing Protection Practices in Greece (HARP); aimed at improving protection activities and mental health support for asylum seekers. Construction of facilities on islands like Samos and Lesvos to provide better living conditions for refugees. Despite these efforts, challenges such as overcrowding in camps and inadequate long term housing solutions persist.

Italy has also received substantial EU funding to manage its refugee population. Projects funded include; initiatives aimed at providing language training and job counseling for refugees and improvements to existing centers to ensure compliance with EU standards. Italy continues to face criticisms regarding its handling of asylum applications and integration processes.

Refugees In Europe

The refugee crisis from the Middle East has been largely driven by conflicts such as the Syrian Civil War, which began in 2011, leading to millions fleeing to Europe. In contrast, the recent influx of Ukrainian refugees is primarily a result of the Russian invasion that started in February 2022. Both crises have been influenced by geopolitical factors; the Middle East's complex political landscape and Ukraine's proximity to EU borders. The geopolitical dynamics surrounding these migrations differ significantly. The EU's response to the Syrian refugee crisis in 2015 was characterized by reluctance and stringent border controls, whereas the Ukrainian crisis prompted an immediate activation of the Temporary Protection Directive (TPD), allowing for expedited support and integration into European societies.

Middle Eastern refugees predominantly come from diverse ethnic backgrounds, including Arabs, Kurds, and others, with Islam as the major religion. In contrast, Ukrainian refugees are largely ethnically Slavic and predominantly Christian. The demographic differences play a crucial role in shaping public perception; Ukrainians are often seen as more culturally similar to Europeans compared to Middle Easterners. These demographic characteristics influence policy responses and public attitudes towards refugees. For instance, positive perceptions of Ukrainians have led to more favorable policies, while negative stereotypes associated with Middle

Eastern refugees have resulted in discriminatory practices.

European law provides various protections for refugees under the 1951 Refugee Convention. However, the application of these laws varies significantly between groups. The TPD activated for Ukrainian refugees grants them rights to work, healthcare, and education without lengthy asylum processes. In contrast, Middle Eastern refugees face bureaucratic hurdles and often experience delays in asylum processing. This discrepancy illustrates a selective application of legal protections based on nationality and perceived cultural affinity. Media representation plays a significant role in shaping public perception. Ukrainian refugees have been portrayed sympathetically in European media as victims of aggression, while Middle Eastern refugees are often depicted through a lens of crisis and threat. This differential portrayal affects public opinion significantly; positive media narratives surrounding Ukrainians foster support for their integration while reinforcing negative stereotypes about Middle Eastern refugees leads to hostility and exclusionary policies.

Case studies from countries like Poland highlight stark contrasts in treatment; Ukrainian refugees receive extensive support services and community integration programs, while Middle Eastern refugees face pushbacks at borders and inadequate housing conditions. Countries such as Germany have implemented robust support systems for Ukrainians but have historically struggled with integrating Middle

Eastern refugees due to political resistance and societal backlash.

Race and religion significantly influence how different refugee groups are treated in Europe. The predominantly Christian identity of Ukrainian refugees aligns more closely with European cultural norms compared to the Islamic identity of many Middle Eastern refugees, leading to preferential treatment for Ukrainians. Discrimination against Middle Eastern refugees is evident in various forms, including physical violence at borders and systemic neglect within asylum systems. Conversely, Ukrainian refugees often experience a welcoming environment due to shared cultural ties with European nations.

Human Rights Violations In The USA

Human rights are fundamental entitlements inherent to all individuals, regardless of nationality, ethnicity, or any other status. In the context of the United States, these rights are enshrined in various legal frameworks, including the Constitution and international treaties. The significance of human rights in the U.S. is profound, as they serve as a foundation for justice, equality, and dignity. Systemic racism refers to the ingrained policies, practices, and cultural norms that perpetuate racial inequality and discrimination within societal structures. In the U.S., systemic racism has had a devastating impact on marginalized communities, particularly African Americans, Indigenous peoples, and other people of color. The historical roots of systemic racism in the U.S. can be traced back to colonial times and have been perpetuated through various laws and policies. The Three-Fifths Compromise (1787) was a constitutional provision that counted enslaved individuals as three-fifths of a person for congressional representation, reinforcing racial hierarchies. Jim Crow Laws were state laws that enforced racial segregation in public facilities, schools, and transportation, institutionalizing discrimination against African Americans.

Brown v. Board of Education (1954) was a landmark Supreme Court decision that declared racial segregation in public schools unconstitutional, marking a significant step towards civil rights. The

Civil Rights Act (1964) was legislation prohibited discrimination based on race, color, religion, sex, or national origin in employment and public accommodations. Despite these advancements, many laws and policies have continued to uphold systemic racism through mechanisms such as voter suppression and economic disenfranchisement.

Redlining is a discriminatory practice that originated in the 1930s when banks and insurers used color-coded maps to determine areas deemed "risky" for investment. Predominantly Black neighborhoods were marked in red, indicating they were undesirable for loans and insurance. Home ownership rates among African Americans plummeted compared to their white counterparts. In 1960, only 27% of Black families owned homes compared to 65% of white families. The lack of access to mortgages prevented many Black families from building wealth through property ownership.

The long-term effects of redlining have created significant economic disadvantages for communities affected by it. Neighborhoods subjected to redlining continue to experience lower property values and reduced access to quality education and healthcare. A study by the National Community Reinvestment Coalition found that neighborhoods historically affected by redlining have seen property values decline by as much as 30% compared to non-redlined areas.

Voter suppression encompasses various tactics aimed at discouraging or preventing specific groups from voting. In recent years, numerous laws have been implemented that disproportionately affect voters of color. Many states require specific forms of identification to vote, which disproportionately impacts minorities who may lack access to these IDs. States often remove individuals from voter rolls based on inactivity or failure to respond to mailings. These practices can lead to eligible voters being disenfranchised. According to a report by the Brennan Center for Justice, states with strict voter ID laws saw a decrease in turnout among Black voters by approximately 20% during elections. Case studies from Georgia highlight how aggressive voter roll purges disproportionately affected African American voters leading up to the 2018 gubernatorial election.

Racial bias within the criminal justice system has led to significant disparities in sentencing between African Americans and their white counterparts. African Americans receive longer sentences than white individuals for similar offenses. For example, a study published by the U.S. Sentencing Commission found that Black men received sentences that were on average 19% longer than those imposed on white men for similar crimes. The War on Drugs has disproportionately targeted communities of color, leading to higher incarceration rates among African Americans despite similar drug usage rates across racial groups.

Discriminatory practices such as denial of mortgages and access to credit have resulted in substantial wealth gaps between races. According to the Federal Reserve, the median net worth of white households is approximately ten times greater than that of Black households. The denial of mortgages based on race has perpetuated cycles of poverty in minority communities while allowing white families to accumulate wealth through home equity.

Studies have shown that Black drivers are significantly more likely to be pulled over than white drivers. According to a report from the American Civil Liberties Union (ACLU), Black drivers are nearly three times more likely to be stopped than white drivers.

In New York City, stop and frisk policies disproportionately targeted Black and Hispanic individuals. Data revealed that in 2011, 87% of those stopped were Black or Hispanic, despite these groups representing a smaller percentage of the city's population.

Mass incarceration refers to the substantial increase in the number of individuals incarcerated in the United States over recent decades, particularly among communities of color. The statistics surrounding mass incarceration are alarming. Black individuals account for approximately 13% of the U.S. population but represent over 60% of those incarcerated. According to the NAACP, one in three Black boys born today can expect to be sentenced to prison at some point in their lives.

The consequences of mass incarceration extend beyond individual sentences. Families are often torn apart due to incarceration, leading to economic instability and emotional trauma. Communities face increased poverty rates as many formerly incarcerated individuals struggle to find employment due to stigma and legal barriers.

Policies initiated during the War on Drugs disproportionately targeted communities of color, leading to harsher sentencing laws for drug-related offenses. Zero tolerance policies which often result in increased arrests for minor infractions in marginalized communities.

Societal attitudes towards race and crime contribute significantly to systemic issues within law enforcement. Stereotypes associating people of color with criminality perpetuate discriminatory practices among law enforcement officials.

Institutional racism is embedded within various systems, including law enforcement agencies. This racism manifests through biased training practices, lack of diversity within police departments, and inadequate accountability measures for officers involved in misconduct.

The Maternal Health Crisis Affecting Black Women In The United States

Human rights violations in the context of health disparities refer to the inequitable access to healthcare, treatment, and outcomes based on race and socioeconomic status. In the United States, these violations are starkly evident in maternal health, where systemic inequities disproportionately affect Black women. Despite advancements in medical technology and healthcare access, Black women face alarming rates of maternal mortality and morbidity compared to their white counterparts.

The maternal health crisis in the United States is characterized by significant disparities in maternal mortality rates between Black women and white women. According to the Centers for Disease Control and Prevention (CDC) in 2021, Black women were three times more likely to die from pregnancy related causes than white women. The maternal mortality rate for Black women was approximately 69.9 deaths per 100,000 live births, compared to 26.6 deaths per 100,000 live births for white women. A report published by the National Institute for Health Care Management found that Black women are more likely to experience severe complications during pregnancy and childbirth, including preeclampsia and hemorrhage. These statistics highlight a critical public health crisis that demands urgent attention and action.

The historical factors contributing to systemic inequities in healthcare for communities of color are deeply rooted in racism and discrimination. Historically, systemic racism has led to economic disadvantages for Black communities. Limited access to quality education and employment opportunities has resulted in lower socioeconomic status, which directly affects health outcomes. Many Black women reside in areas with fewer healthcare resources. Rural or underserved urban areas often lack access to quality prenatal care, leading to increased risks during pregnancy.

The legacy of discrimination in healthcare is evident through practices such as the Tuskegee Syphilis Study and forced sterilizations of Black women. These historical injustices have fostered mistrust in the medical system among Black communities.

Barriers to accessing quality healthcare significantly impact maternal health outcomes for Black women. Black women are more likely to be uninsured or underinsured compared to their white counterparts. According to the Kaiser Family Foundation, approximately 10% of Black women are uninsured compared to 6% of white women.

The absence of culturally competent care contributes to poor health outcomes. Many healthcare providers lack training on the unique needs and experiences of Black women, leading to misunderstandings and inadequate treatment.

Nike Inc.

Nike, Inc. is a leading global brand in athletic footwear and apparel, renowned for its innovative products and marketing prowess. Founded in 1964 as Blue Ribbon Sports and rebranded in 1971, Nike has grown to become the largest supplier of athletic shoes and apparel worldwide, generating over $46 billion in revenue in 2022. However, the company has faced significant allegations regarding human rights violations, particularly concerning child labor practices in its supply chain.

In the 1990s reports began surfacing about poor working conditions in Nike's factories, particularly in Southeast Asia. Activist groups highlighted these issues, prompting media coverage. In 1996 the first major report from the organization Global Exchange accused Nike of using child labor in its factories in Vietnam and Indonesia. In 1998 a report by Human Rights Watch documented instances of child labor in Nike's supply chain, including children working long hours for low wages. Protests erupted against Nike during the Sydney Olympics, where activists called attention to labor abuses linked to the brand. By the 2010s continued scrutiny led to further commitments from Nike regarding transparency and labor practices. However, sporadic reports of child labor persisted.

Several key incidents have brought attention to child labor practices associated with Nike. In 1997, a report revealed that children as young as 10 were working in factories producing Nike products in Vietnam. In

2001, investigations found that children were involved in making soccer balls for Nike in Indonesia, often working under hazardous conditions.

Vietnam and Indonesia have historically faced socio-economic challenges that contribute to child labor practices. Vietnam underwent significant economic reforms known as "Doi Moi" starting in the late 1980s, transitioning from a centrally planned economy to a socialist-oriented market economy. While this led to economic growth, it also resulted in increased exploitation of workers, including children who were often forced into labor due to family poverty.

Indonesia's economic landscape has been characterized by high levels of unemployment and underemployment. Many families rely on the income generated by their children working in factories or informal sectors, perpetuating a cycle of poverty.

These socio-economic factors create an environment where child labor becomes a viable option for families struggling to make ends meet.

Apple's Complicity In Child Labor Practices In Cobalt Mines of The DRC

Human rights violations in global supply chains refer to the exploitation and mistreatment of workers, often in developing countries, where labor laws may be weak or poorly enforced. These violations can include child labor, forced labor, and unsafe working conditions. Apple Inc., a leading technology company known for its innovative products such as the iPhone and MacBook, has been at the forefront of the tech industry since its founding in 1976. However, the company has faced serious allegations regarding its complicity in child labor practices within cobalt mines in the Democratic Republic of Congo (DRC).

The DRC is home to over 70% of the world's cobalt reserves, a critical mineral used in lithium-ion batteries that power many electronic devices, including smartphones and laptops. Cobalt mining in the DRC is often characterized by artisanal mining practices, where individuals and families extract cobalt from small scale mines, sometimes using rudimentary tools. Cobalt is essential for battery production due to its ability to enhance energy density and stability. As demand for electric vehicles and portable electronics continues to rise, so does the need for cobalt. This demand has led to increased mining activities in the DRC, often without adequate oversight or regulation.

The DRC faces significant socioeconomic challenges, including widespread poverty, political instability, and inadequate access to education. Many families rely on the income generated from child labor in cobalt mines to survive. Children are often compelled to work long hours under hazardous conditions, sacrificing their education and well-being for financial support.

Apple has been accused of indirectly supporting child labor practices through its supply chain for cobalt sourcing. Reports from various NGOs have highlighted these allegations. Amnesty International reported that children as young as seven years old work in hazardous conditions in DRC's cobalt mines, often without protective equipment. The report specifically mentioned that Apple's suppliers sourced cobalt from these mines. The Washington Post published an article detailing how children are exposed to dangerous working conditions while mining cobalt for companies that supply major tech firms like Apple. These allegations raise serious concerns about children's rights and safety, as they are subjected to physical risks and denied access to education.

Child Labor In Cobalt Mining And The Involvement of Tesla And Apple

Human rights violations, particularly concerning child labor, have become a significant concern in the technology industry, especially as companies increasingly rely on minerals sourced from regions with weak labor protections. Tesla and Apple are two major players in the electric vehicle and technology markets, respectively, both of which utilize cobalt; a crucial component in battery production. Cobalt is an essential element in lithium-ion batteries, which power a vast array of electronic devices, including smartphones, laptops, and electric vehicles. The demand for cobalt has surged with the rise of electric vehicles (EVs) and renewable energy technologies, making it a critical resource for companies like Tesla and Apple.

The Democratic Republic of Congo (DRC) is the world's largest producer of cobalt, supplying 70% of the global market. Cobalt mining in the DRC often involves artisanal mining practices, where individuals extract minerals using basic tools. These operations are frequently unregulated and lack safety measures, leading to dangerous working conditions. Child labor is a pervasive issue in DRC's cobalt mining sector. Reports indicate that thousands of children work in mines under hazardous conditions, often for minimal pay. They are exposed to physical dangers such as cave-ins and toxic substances while missing out on education and childhood development.

Tesla has faced scrutiny over its supply chain practices concerning cobalt sourcing. Investigations have revealed that Tesla sources cobalt from suppliers linked to mines known for child labor practices. For instance, reports from organizations like Amnesty International have highlighted that some cobalt used in Tesla batteries originate from artisanal mines where children work. Tesla has not been sufficiently transparent about its sourcing practices and the steps taken to ensure that its supply chain is free from child labor. These allegations raise significant concerns regarding Tesla's commitment to ethical sourcing and corporate responsibility.

Apple has also faced serious allegations regarding child labor in its supply chain. Like Tesla, Apple has been accused of sourcing cobalt from suppliers linked to child labor practices in the DRC. Reports from organizations such as Human Rights Watch have documented instances where children work in hazardous conditions to extract cobalt used in Apple products.

While both companies have publicly committed to ethical sourcing, their responses have differed. Apple has established a Supplier Code of Conduct and conducts regular audits of its suppliers. In contrast, Tesla's response has been criticized for lacking sufficient detail regarding its supply chain oversight.

Child Labor In The Supply Chain of General Mills

Human rights violations encompass a range of abuses that infringe upon the fundamental rights and freedoms of individuals. In the context of corporate ethics, these violations are particularly significant as companies navigate their responsibilities within global supply chains. General Mills, a prominent player in the food industry known for products like Cheerios, has faced scrutiny over its supply chain practices, particularly regarding child labor.

Child labor remains a pervasive issue worldwide, with an estimated 160 million children engaged in child labor as of 2020, according to the International Labour Organization (ILO). This figure represents a significant portion of children working in hazardous conditions, particularly in industries such as agriculture and manufacturing. The food industry is not exempt from these practices, with reports indicating that children are often employed illegally to meet labor demands in various sectors.

Several international conventions aim to combat child labor and protect children's rights. The UN Convention on the Rights of the Child (CRC) emphasizes that children should be protected from economic exploitation and work that is hazardous or detrimental to their education and development. Additionally, the ILO's Minimum Age Convention (No. 138) sets the minimum age for employment at 15 years, with stricter regulations for hazardous work.

Reports from various organizations have highlighted instances of child labor in factories supplying General Mills products. Investigations have revealed that some subcontractors engaged by General Mills have employed children illegally, particularly in regions where labor laws are poorly enforced. For example, a report by Human Rights Watch detailed how children were found working in unsafe conditions while producing ingredients for popular cereals. Regions most affected by child labor in the supply chain of General Mills include parts of South Asia and Africa, where poverty and lack of access to education drive families to rely on their children's income. Socio-economic factors such as limited job opportunities and inadequate enforcement of labor laws contribute significantly to the prevalence of child labor in these areas.

Child labor often prevents children from attending school, limiting their future opportunities and perpetuating cycles of poverty. Working long hours in hazardous conditions poses serious health risks, including physical injuries and exposure to harmful substances. The stress and trauma associated with exploitation can lead to long term psychological issues, affecting children's overall well-being. The broader implications of child labor extend beyond individual children. Societies that allow child labor may experience stunted economic growth due to a less educated workforce. Furthermore, reliance on exploitative practices undermines efforts toward sustainable development and social equity.

Cargill And Child Labor In Cocoa Production

Cargill has been involved in cocoa production for several decades, sourcing cocoa beans primarily from West Africa, which is responsible for approximately 70% of the world's cocoa supply. The company operates across the entire cocoa supply chain, from sourcing and processing to distribution. Cargill's significant presence in this sector makes it a key player in determining labor practices and standards within the industry. The cocoa supply chain involves multiple stages, including farming, harvesting, fermenting, drying, and transporting cocoa beans. West Africa is crucial to this supply chain due to its favorable climate for cocoa cultivation. Countries like Cote d'Ivoire and Ghana are among the largest producers of cocoa globally. Unfortunately, these regions also face challenges such as poverty and lack of educational opportunities, contributing to the prevalence of child labor.

Cargill has been accused of complicity in child labor practices on cocoa farms that supply its products. Reports from organizations such as UNICEF and the International Labour Organization (ILO) indicate that children as young as six years old work on cocoa farms under hazardous conditions. Children are often involved in dangerous tasks such as using machetes for harvesting cocoa pods or carrying heavy loads. Many children working on these farms do not attend school, limiting their future opportunities.

According to a 2020 report by UNICEF, approximately 1.5 million children were engaged in child labor in cocoa production across West Africa. Investigations have documented specific cases where children were found working on farms linked to Cargill's supply chain. For instance, a report by Human Rights Watch highlighted instances where children were discovered working long hours without proper safety measures or education.

Consumers are encouraged to educate themselves about the origins of their chocolate products and support brands that prioritize ethical sourcing practices. By advocating for fair trade and holding corporations accountable for their supply chains, individuals can contribute significantly to eradicating child labor globally.

Labor Practices In Hyundai And Kia's Supply Chains

The automotive industry plays a pivotal role in the global economy, contributing significantly to employment and technological advancements. However, this industry also faces substantial ethical responsibilities, particularly regarding labor practices within its supply chains. Recent allegations against Hyundai and Kia have brought to light serious concerns about child labor in factories supplying parts for their vehicles. Reports indicate that children as young as 12 years old have been employed in hazardous conditions, raising questions about corporate accountability and ethical labor standards.

Recent investigations have uncovered alarming instances of child labor within the supply chains of Hyundai and Kia. A notable case involved a 13 year old girl who worked up to 60 hours per week at a supplier factory in Alabama, which produces components for Hyundai vehicles. Reports indicate that at least four major suppliers employed underage workers, with the U.S. Department of Labor actively investigating these violations. Statistics reveal a troubling trend; the number of minors illegally employed in the U.S. has surged by 152% from 2018 to 2023, highlighting systemic issues within manufacturing sectors.

The legal landscape surrounding child labor varies significantly across countries. In the U.S., federal laws strictly prohibit the employment of minors in hazardous occupations, yet enforcement can be inconsistent, particularly in states with weaker labor regulations. Internationally, organizations such as the International Labour Organization (ILO) set standards aimed at eradicating child labor. The ethical implications of employing child labor are profound; it not only violates basic human rights but also undermines the integrity of corporate social responsibility initiatives.

Doe v. Boy Scouts of America Case

The Doe v. Boy Scouts of America case is a landmark legal proceeding that highlights critical issues surrounding child protection and organizational responsibility. The case centers on allegations of sexual abuse against a minor by a scout leader, raising significant questions about the Boy Scouts of America's (BSA) duty to protect its members. This case is particularly significant in the context of increasing scrutiny on youth organizations and their accountability in safeguarding vulnerable populations.

Historically, the Boy Scouts of America has been a prominent youth organization in the United States, particularly during the 1970s when it was at its peak in membership and influence. However, this period also saw increasing reports of inappropriate behavior by adult leaders. In the Doe case, the plaintiff alleged that he was sexually abused by his scout leader, Siegfried Hepp, between 1975 and 1977. The BSA was accused of having prior knowledge of Hepp's inappropriate conduct but failed to take adequate measures to protect scouts from him. Evidence presented during the trial indicated that BSA maintained "ineligible volunteer files," which documented past allegations against leaders like Hepp but were not acted upon effectively.

In this case, legal definitions of negligence and liability are crucial. Negligence refers to the failure to exercise reasonable care, resulting in harm to another party. Liability pertains to the legal responsibility for such harm. Relevant laws include state statutes governing child protection and organizational accountability, such as mandatory reporting laws that require organizations to report suspected abuse to authorities. The BSA's failure to act on known risks associated with scout leaders raises questions about its adherence to these laws and its overall duty of care towards its members.

The trial featured compelling testimonies from Doe, who recounted his experiences of abuse, alongside testimonies from BSA representatives who attempted to distance the organization from responsibility. The jury deliberated on the evidence presented, ultimately awarding Doe $11.8 million in damages; one of the largest sums awarded in similar cases against BSA. The jury's decision was influenced by findings that BSA had acted recklessly by allowing known abusers access to children.

Lewis v. Boy Scouts of America

The case of Kerry Lewis against the BSA emerged from a troubling history of abuse within the organization, highlighting critical issues of legal accountability and organizational responsibility. This case is significant not only for its legal precedents but also for its broader societal impact on child protection policies within youth organizations.

Kerry Lewis's lawsuit against the BSA stems from his experiences as a scout in the 1980s, where he was sexually abused by scout leader Timur Dykes. Dykes had a documented history of inappropriate behavior and had previously confessed to abusing boys in scouting. Despite this knowledge, BSA's organizational policies failed to effectively protect minors from known offenders. During the 1980s, there was a broader context of abuse within youth organizations, with many institutions struggling to address allegations and protect children adequately.

The BSA's internal policies regarding the protection of minors were insufficient, as evidenced by their failure to act on reports about Dykes. This negligence contributed to an environment where abuse could occur without accountability. The systemic issues within BSA reflected a troubling trend in youth organizations during this era, where many institutions prioritized reputation over the safety of children.

Kerry Lewis's lawsuit against the BSA was grounded in claims of negligence and failure to protect minors from known abusers. The legal basis for his claims included allegations that the BSA had a duty of care to safeguard its members but failed to take appropriate action when informed about Dykes's abusive behavior. The defense strategies employed by BSA included denying knowledge of Dykes's past abuses and arguing that they had no actual duty of care towards Lewis. Relevant laws governing child protection and organizational liability include various state statutes that mandate reporting suspected abuse and outline the responsibilities organizations have towards their members. The failure to adhere to these regulations can result in significant legal consequences for organizations like the BSA.

During the trial, key arguments were presented by both the plaintiff and the defense. Lewis's legal team emphasized the emotional and psychological trauma he suffered due to BSA's negligence in allowing Dykes continued access to scouts despite prior allegations. Conversely, BSA's defense focused on denying knowledge of any misconduct and attempting to shift responsibility away from themselves. The jury's deliberation process took into account evidence presented regarding BSA's internal documents that indicated prior knowledge of Dykes's behavior. Ultimately, the jury awarded Lewis $18.5 million in damages, reflecting their determination that BSA had acted negligently and recklessly in its duty to protect young scouts.

The Perversion Files

The Boy Scouts of America (BSA), founded in 1910, is one of the largest youth organizations in the United States, with a mission to instill values of citizenship, character development, and personal fitness in young people. The release of over 20,000 pages of allegations against scout leaders, known as the "Perversion Files," has drawn significant attention and scrutiny toward the organization. These files document numerous cases of sexual abuse by adult leaders, raising critical questions about BSA's commitment to child protection and organizational accountability.

Historically, the BSA has faced various challenges regarding its leadership and child protection policies. In the 1980s, growing awareness of sexual abuse within youth organizations prompted the BSA to develop its Youth Protection program, which aimed to educate leaders and prevent abuse. Notable events leading to scrutiny include the Kerry Lewis v. Boy Scouts of America case in 2010, where a former scout alleged he was abused by a scout leader who had previously confessed to molesting other boys. This case highlighted systemic failures within BSA to protect its members and manage known offenders effectively.

The "Perversion Files" consist of confidential documents maintained by the BSA that detail allegations of sexual abuse by scout leaders from 1965 to 1985. The files reveal over 1,200 cases involving various types of misconduct, including inappropriate touching and sexual assault. Profiles of the accused leaders often indicate a troubling pattern; many were allowed to continue working with scouts despite prior allegations or confessions. The files suggest a systemic issue within the organization where protecting its reputation took precedence over safeguarding children. Analysis of the Perversion Files uncovers alarming patterns of abuse and organizational cover-up. Many incidents were not reported to law enforcement, with BSA officials often opting for internal handling rather than public disclosure. In some cases, abusers were simply moved to different locations or roles within the organization rather than being removed entirely. For example, Timur Dykes, who confessed to molesting multiple boys in the early 1980s, continued to serve as a scout leader for years after his admissions. This pattern indicates a culture within BSA that prioritized its image over accountability and victim protection.

The psychological and social effects on victims of abuse within scouting can be profound and long lasting. Survivors often experience trauma that manifests as anxiety, depression, and difficulties in forming trusting relationships. Testimonies from victims reveal feelings of betrayal not only by their abusers but also by an organization that failed to protect them. Case studies illustrate how these experiences have led many survivors to seek justice through legal avenues, contributing to a broader movement advocating for child protection reforms.

The Catholic Church And The Holocaust

The Catholic Church has historically wielded significant influence in Europe, particularly in Germany, where it shaped social and moral norms throughout the 20th century. However, during the Holocaust, as Nazi Germany rose to power and initiated its campaign of genocide against Jews and other minorities, the Church's response has been a subject of intense scrutiny. The release of over 20,000 pages of allegations against church leaders highlights a troubling legacy of complicity, silence, and even assistance in the escape of Nazi officials post-war.

Before 1933, the Catholic Church held a prominent position in German society, influencing both public opinion and political landscapes. The Reichskonkordat, signed in 1933 between the Vatican and Nazi Germany, was intended to protect the rights of Catholics in Germany but has been criticized for effectively legitimizing the Nazi regime. Despite initial hopes for cooperation, tensions soon arose as the Nazis began persecuting clergy and laity alike. The relationship between the Church and Nazi ideology was complex; while some church leaders condemned aspects of Nazi policy, many others remained silent or complicit due to opportunism.

Numerous instances reveal how church leaders or institutions were complicit in the persecution of Jews and other minorities during the Holocaust. For example, Cardinal Augustus Hlond in Poland openly supported non-violent anti-Jewish discrimination while other bishops remained silent about the escalating violence against Jews. Analysis of church documents from this period indicates that while some clergy did speak out against Nazi policies, many chose silence or passive acceptance instead.

In regions like France and Poland, local church authorities often failed to protect Jewish congregants. In many cases, churches were used as venues for anti-Semitic propaganda rather than as sanctuaries for those seeking refuge. This complicity is further illustrated by specific case studies that highlight how church institutions either ignored or actively supported discriminatory laws against Jews. The Catholic Church's public stance during the Holocaust is marked by a notable lack of condemnation regarding Nazi atrocities. Prominent figures within the Church, including Pope Pius XII, have been criticized for their silence. While some bishops courageously denounced deportations, such as the Dutch bishops who issued letters against the deportation of Jews, many others refrained from taking a stand due to political motivations or fear of repercussions from the Nazis. This silence can be attributed to an underlying anti-Semitic sentiment that had persisted within certain segments of the Church.

Post war investigations have unveiled networks established by members of the Catholic Church aimed at aiding Nazi officials in escaping prosecution. Notably, many Nazis were provided with false documents or facilitated routes through Italy to reach safe havens in South America. This assistance raises profound ethical questions about the Church's moral standing during and after the war. Church officials often justified their actions by claiming they were protecting individuals from unjust persecution; however, this rationale does little to absolve them from complicity in aiding perpetrators of genocide. The implications of these actions continue to resonate within discussions about accountability and moral responsibility.

The World Council of Churches In The 1970s

The World Council of Churches (WCC) was established in 1948, emerging from the ecumenical movement aimed at promoting unity among Christian denominations. By the 1970s, the WCC had grown significantly, representing a diverse array of member churches from various geopolitical contexts. Its mission was to foster dialogue and cooperation among Christian communities while addressing pressing social issues, including poverty, war, and human rights abuses. The socio-political landscape of the 1970s was marked by the Cold War's ideological divide, with many Eastern European countries under communist regimes. This period saw increasing tensions between Western and Eastern blocs, leading to widespread human rights violations in countries such as Poland, Czechoslovakia, and Hungary. The WCC sought to engage with these issues but faced significant challenges in advocating for human rights within oppressive political environments.

Throughout the 1970s, the WCC faced criticism regarding its handling of human rights abuses in communist countries. Critics argued that the organization was either too lenient or ineffective in addressing the plight of persecuted individuals. Member churches from Western nations often accused the WCC of failing to adequately support dissidents and human rights advocates in Eastern Europe. Human rights organizations also expressed frustration with the WCC's approach. They contended that the Council's emphasis on dialogue and reconciliation sometimes led to a reluctance to confront oppressive regimes directly. Dissidents within Eastern Europe criticized the WCC for its perceived complicity through silence or inaction regarding state sponsored violence and persecution.

Claims of complicity emerged as critics argued that the WCC's engagement with communist regimes undermined its credibility as a champion of human rights. By prioritizing dialogue over direct confrontation, some stakeholders believed that the Council inadvertently legitimized oppressive governments. This perception strained relationships with member churches that were more directly affected by state repression, leading to tensions within the ecumenical community.

The actions and inactions of the WCC during this period had lasting implications for its reputation as a global ecumenical body. While it successfully facilitated dialogue among member churches and raised awareness about social justice issues, criticisms regarding its effectiveness in addressing human rights violations persisted. In subsequent decades, these criticisms influenced policy shifts within the WCC, prompting a more robust commitment to advocating for human rights globally.

The Croatian War of Independence

The Croatian War of Independence (1991-1995) was a pivotal conflict that arose after Croatia declared independence from the Socialist Federal Republic of Yugoslavia. This war was characterized by intense fighting between Croatian forces and the Serb controlled Yugoslav People's Army, resulting in significant casualties and displacement on both sides. The Croatian Catholic Church played a crucial role in this socio-political landscape, acting as a significant influence on national identity and political sentiments during the tumultuous 1990s. The Croatian Catholic Church, while presenting itself as a moral authority, was implicated in supporting nationalist forces that engaged in ethnic cleansing against Serbs during the war. Through its actions and statements, the Church fostered an environment conducive to these nationalist agendas, which had lasting implications for inter-ethnic relations in Croatia.

The relationship between the Croatian Catholic Church and the Croatian state has deep historical roots, dating back to the Austro-Hungarian period when Catholicism was recognized as a state religion. Throughout history, the Church has been intertwined with national identity formation, often acting as a unifying force for Croats against perceived external threats, particularly from Serbs. Leading up to the war, nationalism surged in Croatia, fueled by historical grievances and a desire for self-determination. The Church's involvement in this nationalism can be traced back to its role in promoting Croatian identity during past conflicts, such as World War II, when it aligned with nationalist movements.

During the war, official statements from the Croatian Catholic Church largely supported the government's stance on independence and territorial integrity. High ranking church leaders often echoed government rhetoric, framing Serb controlled areas as occupied territories. Notably, Cardinal Franjo Kuharic's public statements frequently aligned with military actions taken by Croatian forces, including Operation Storm in 1995, which was portrayed as a legitimate liberation of Croatian land. Documented instances reveal that some church leaders expressed satisfaction with military successes against Serbs and criticized Western responses to these actions. The Church's publications often rejected allegations of war crimes and ethnic cleansing associated with Croatian forces.

Ethnic cleansing is defined as the systematic removal or extermination of an ethnic group from a territory. During the Croatian War of Independence, numerous allegations emerged regarding atrocities committed against Serbs. Reports indicated that nationalist forces engaged in forced displacement, killings, and other acts aimed at creating ethnically homogeneous territories. Evidence supporting these allegations includes testimonies from survivors, reports from international observers, and analyses by academic scholars. The role of the Church in fostering an atmosphere that enabled such actions is critical to understanding these dynamics. By legitimizing nationalist sentiments and downplaying violence against Serbs, the Church contributed to an environment where ethnic cleansing could occur with minimal opposition.

The Croatian Catholic Church significantly influenced national identity during the war by promoting a narrative that framed Croats as victims fighting for their homeland against aggressors. This narrative solidified ethnic divisions and fostered animosity towards Serbs, complicating post-war reconciliation efforts. The implications of this contribution were profound; inter-ethnic relations deteriorated sharply during and after the conflict. The long term effects include ongoing tensions between Croats and Serbs in contemporary Croatia, where historical grievances continue to shape political discourse.

The Catholic Church In The 1994 Rwanda Genocide

The Rwandan genocide, which occurred over a span of approximately 100 days from April to July 1994, resulted in the brutal slaughter of an estimated 800,000 Tutsis and moderate Hutus. The socio-political landscape of Rwanda in the early 1990s was marked by ethnic tensions exacerbated by colonial legacies and political manipulation. The Catholic Church held a prominent position within Rwandan society, with a majority of the population identifying as Catholic. This influence extended into both political and social spheres, making the Church a powerful entity capable of shaping public opinion and moral direction.

Research on the Catholic Church's involvement in the Rwandan genocide reveals a complex interplay between complicity and resistance. Key authors such as Timothy Longman and Peter Celestine Safari have documented instances where clergy members actively participated in or condoned violence against Tutsis. Conversely, some studies highlight efforts by individual church members to protect victims. This dichotomy underscores varying perspectives on the Church's role, with debates centering around institutional accountability versus individual actions.

Evidence indicates that certain clergy members directly participated in violence against Tutsis, with documented cases of incitement and support for Hutu militias. For instance, some priests provided lists of Tutsi individuals seeking refuge in churches to militia groups, leading to their subsequent murder. Furthermore, systemic issues within the Church, such as theological justifications for violence and strong loyalties to political regimes, contributed significantly to its inaction during the genocide.

Simeon Ben Yohai on Sexual Intercourse With Minors In Talmudic Literature

Simeon Ben Yohai, a prominent Talmudic sage of the 2nd century CE, is revered for his contributions to Jewish thought, particularly in the areas of law and ethics. His teachings are integral to understanding the complexities of sexual ethics within Talmudic literature. The Talmudic period was characterized by distinct societal norms regarding minors and sexuality. In ancient Jewish society, marriage at a young age was not uncommon, often viewed as a means of securing familial alliances and ensuring economic stability. However, this practice raises significant ethical concerns when examined through a modern lens. These societal norms likely influenced the perspectives of Jewish sages, including Ben Yohai. The tension between legal recognition of child marriage and the ethical implications of such practices is evident in Talmudic discourse. Scholars argue that while some sages may have accepted child marriage as a social norm, others expressed concern over its potential for exploitation and abuse.

Several passages in the Talmud reflect Simeon Ben Yohai's views on sexual relations with minors. One notable reference is found in ***Kethuboth 11b;*** (Although the intercourse of a small boy is not regarded as a sexual act, nevertheless the woman is injured by it as by a piece of wood), where it is stated that "when a grown man has intercourse with a little girl, it is nothing." This statement has been interpreted by some scholars as indicative of a permissive attitude toward such relationships. In another passage from ***Niddah 44b;*** *(*A girl who is three years and one day old, whose father arranged her betrothal, is betrothed through intercourse, as the halakhic status of intercourse with her is that of intercourse in all halakhic senses. And in a case where the childless husband of a girl three years and one day old dies, if his brother the yavam engages in intercourse with her, he acquires her as his wife; and if she is married, a man other than her husband is liable for engaging in intercourse with her due to violation of the prohibition against intercourse with a married woman*.)*; the discussion surrounding sexual activity with minors highlights the complexities involved. The text suggests that while such acts may not carry the same halakhic ramifications as those involving adults, they nonetheless raise significant ethical concerns regarding consent and agency.

Translations of these texts reveal a stark contrast between the historical acceptance of certain practices and contemporary ethical standards that categorically reject any form of sexual activity involving minors. The interpretations of Simeon Ben Yohai's statements have sparked considerable debate among scholars. Some contemporary commentators argue that his views reflect an understanding of minors as vulnerable individuals who require protection from exploitation. Others contend that his permissive statements may inadvertently normalize harmful practices. Ethical implications arise from these interpretations, particularly regarding how they inform modern discussions about consent and the rights of minors. Scholars emphasize the need to critically engage with these texts to understand their impact on contemporary Jewish law and ethics.

US Influence on Africa's Adoption of Genetically Modified Organisms (GMOs)

Before the introduction of GMOs, Africa's agricultural landscape was characterized by diverse traditional farming practices. Subsistence farming was predominant, with farmers relying on indigenous seeds and methods suited to local conditions. The introduction of GMOs in Africa was significantly influenced by international organizations and US agricultural policies that promoted biotechnology as a solution to food insecurity. This push often came through bilateral aid and trade agreements that favored GMO adoption, aligning with corporate interests from major agribusinesses like Monsanto and Bayer.

Scientific studies have raised concerns about the health risks associated with GMO seedlings. Research indicates potential links between GMO consumption and health issues, including increased levels of carcinogenic substances in the body. For instance, studies have documented adverse health outcomes in populations consuming GM crops, leading to calls for more rigorous safety evaluations before widespread adoption. Case studies from countries like Zambia have highlighted negative health impacts attributed to GMO maize consumption, emphasizing the need for caution in regulatory practices.

The reliance on US supplied GMO seeds has created economic dependency for many African nations. This dependency is compounded by legal challenges surrounding seed patents and usage rights, which often favor multinational corporations over local farmers. Farmers face lawsuits for patent infringement when using saved seeds from GMO crops, leading to financial strain and loss of autonomy. This situation raises critical questions about agricultural sovereignty and the long term sustainability of such dependency.

Countries such as South Africa, Kenya, and Burkina Faso have prominently adopted GMOs. In South Africa, approximately 90% of maize grown is genetically modified; however, farmers report challenges such as rising costs associated with patented seeds. Testimonies from local farmers reveal mixed feelings about GMOs; while some appreciate increased yields, others express concerns over health risks and economic pressures from seed suppliers. US agricultural policies have been instrumental in promoting GMOs in Africa. These policies often prioritize corporate interests underpinned by international trade agreements that limit African nations' ability to regulate GMO use independently. The influence of these agreements raises concerns about African agricultural sovereignty and the capacity to make autonomous decisions regarding food security.

Modern Day Colonialism

Modern day colonialism refers to the ongoing practices and structures that perpetuate inequalities reminiscent of historical colonialism, particularly in the context of global citizenship and mobility. It manifests through various mechanisms, including economic exploitation, cultural dominance, and political control. One significant aspect of this phenomenon is the hierarchy of passports, which determines individuals' ability to travel, work, and access opportunities worldwide. The historical roots of passport power can be traced back to colonial practices that privileged certain nations over others, creating a legacy that continues to influence global mobility today.

Existing research on passport rankings highlights the significant impact these rankings have on global mobility. The Henley Passport Index, for instance, ranks passports based on the number of destinations their holders can access without a visa. Studies indicate a stark contrast between passports from developed nations, which typically allow visa free access to a majority of countries, and those from developing nations, which often face stringent visa requirements. Theories of colonialism and post-colonialism provide a framework for understanding how historical power dynamics continue to shape contemporary global relations. Scholars like Edward Said and Frantz Fanon have examined how colonial legacies persist in modern governance and societal structures. Research has also explored the socioeconomic consequences of passport strength, revealing how disparities in mobility contribute to broader patterns of inequality.

Data from various sources, including the Henley Passport Index and the Passport Index, illustrate the disparities in passport power between developed and developing nations. As of 2024, passports from countries like Japan, Singapore, France, Germany, and Italy rank at the top, allowing access to 194 destinations without a visa. In contrast, passports from countries such as Afghanistan or Syria rank among the lowest, granting access to merely 28 or 29 destinations. Developed nations typically enjoy extensive visa free travel options, facilitating international business and education opportunities. Conversely, citizens from developing countries often face barriers that limit their ability to travel freely for work or study. These disparities have profound implications for individuals from developing nations regarding their ability to engage in international travel, pursue educational opportunities abroad, or seek employment in more prosperous regions.

Several case studies highlight the barriers faced by individuals from developing countries due to their passport strength. Refugees often encounter significant obstacles when attempting to seek asylum or migrate due to restrictive visa policies tied to their home countries' passports. For instance, refugees from war torn regions may find it nearly impossible to obtain visas for safer nations despite dire circumstances. Professionals from developing nations frequently face challenges in obtaining work visas in developed countries. For example, an IT professional from Nigeria may possess qualifications equivalent to those of a candidate from Canada but may be denied opportunities due solely to passport related restrictions.

The hierarchy of passports contributes significantly to economic inequality and perpetuates colonial dynamics. Countries with powerful passports often maintain control over international agreements that favor their citizens while imposing strict visa requirements on individuals from developing nations. This practice reinforces economic disparities by limiting access to markets and opportunities. The role of powerful nations in shaping visa policies further entrenches these inequalities. For instance, many Western countries implement policies that prioritize applicants from certain regions while excluding others based on perceived risks associated with specific nationalities. Such practices not only hinder individual potential but also reinforce broader patterns of dependency and inequality between nations.

The Thiaroye Massacre

During World War II, Senegalese troops, known as Tirailleurs Senegalais, played a significant role in the defense of France. These soldiers were part of a long tradition of colonial infantry that served France from the mid-19th century onward. Their contributions included fighting valiantly in key battles such as the Battle of France in 1940 and the liberation of southern France in 1944. However, their service was overshadowed by a tragic event; the Thiaroye massacre on December 1st 1944, where over 400 Senegalese soldiers were killed by French forces.

The socio-political climate in France during and after World War II was marked by upheaval and transformation. The war had devastated the nation, leading to significant military and civilian casualties. In this context, Senegalese troops were recruited under dire conditions, often motivated by promises of better wages and opportunities. The Tirailleurs Senegalais had been integral to French military efforts throughout the war, yet they faced systemic discrimination and were often treated as second class soldiers. After the liberation of France, many Senegalese soldiers returned to their homeland only to find themselves in dire circumstances. They were repatriated to Thiaroye military camp near Dakar, where they awaited demobilization and payment for their service. However, delays in wage payments led to rising tensions among the troops. The Thiaroye massacre stemmed from a series of events that culminated in a violent confrontation between Senegalese soldiers and French authorities. On November 25th 1944, Senegalese troops at Thiaroye refused to leave their camp until their unpaid wages were settled. This act of defiance was met with hostility from French military leadership. On December 1st French forces attempted to quell what they labeled a mutiny. Reports indicate that tensions escalated when shots were fired by the French. The French response was brutal; soldiers armed with rifles and backed by artillery opened fire on unarmed Senegalese troops, resulting in the deaths of at least 400 individuals. This tragic event highlighted not only the disregard for the lives of colonial soldiers but also the deep seated racial prejudices within the French military hierarchy.

The immediate aftermath of the Thiaroye massacre was devastating for both the surviving soldiers. Many Senegalese veterans were left traumatized by the violence they had experienced from those they had fought alongside during the war. The massacre also sparked outrage within Senegal and among other African nations, leading to a reevaluation of Franco-African relations.

Racial Foundations of The Transatlantic Slave Trade

The Transatlantic Slave Trade refers to the forced transportation of enslaved Africans to the Americas between the 15th and 19th centuries, marking one of the most tragic chapters in human history. This trade emerged in the context of European colonization and the burgeoning plantation economies in the New World, where labor demands led to a systematic exploitation of African populations. Unlike other forms of slavery practiced globally, which were often based on factors such as debt, warfare, or social status, the Transatlantic Slave Trade was fundamentally rooted in racial ideologies that dehumanized individuals based solely on their African heritage.

The origins of the Transatlantic Slave Trade can be traced back to European exploration and colonization efforts in Africa. Beginning in the 15th century, European powers established coastal slave trading posts and engaged local African leaders to facilitate the capture and sale of enslaved individuals. Key nations involved included Portugal, Britain, Spain, France, and the Netherlands, with Britain emerging as a dominant force by the 18th century.

Statistical estimates indicate that approximately 12 million Africans were forcibly transported across the Atlantic Ocean during this period. The Middle Passage, a harrowing journey characterized by overcrowding and high mortality rates, saw nearly 2 million individuals perish en route due to disease, malnutrition, and brutal conditions.

The emergence of racial theories in Europe during this era played a crucial role in justifying the enslavement of Africans. These ideologies were often intertwined with religious beliefs and pseudo-scientific notions that posited racial superiority. For instance, Europeans constructed narratives that depicted Africans as inferior beings, which facilitated their subjugation under a guise of civilizing missions. In contrast to other global slavery practices, such as those in ancient Rome or Arabian Peninsula, where enslavement was often linked to war or economic status, the racial underpinnings of Transatlantic slavery created a system where enslaved people were permanently defined by their race. This racialized framework not only justified their exploitation but also laid the groundwork for enduring social hierarchies based on race.

Globally, slavery has manifested in various forms across different cultures and epochs. In regions such as Africa and Asia, systems of slavery were frequently predicated on debt or warfare rather than race. In many African societies, individuals could become enslaved due to debt or as a result of warfare but could often regain their freedom. In contrast, systems like those found in ancient Rome allowed for social mobility among enslaved individuals based on merit or service. These non-racially based practices highlight significant differences in how societies structured their labor systems compared to the racially defined chattel slavery seen in the Americas.

The racially based nature of the Transatlantic Slave Trade had profound implications for societal structures in the Americas. It fostered a caste system where race dictated social status and economic opportunity. The cultural ramifications were equally significant; enslaved Africans contributed richly to American culture while simultaneously facing systemic oppression and violence. Furthermore, the legacy of this racial foundation continues to resonate today, influencing contemporary discussions around race relations and systemic inequality within American society.

Human Rights Violations And The Impact on Palestinian Women And Girls

The formation of Israel in 1948 was marked by significant legal and social upheaval, leading to the displacement of hundreds of thousands of Palestinians; a period known as the Nakba. The legal frameworks established during this time have evolved but often perpetuate inequality. The ongoing occupation of Palestinian territories since 1967 has resulted in a dual legal system where Israeli settlers enjoy extensive rights while Palestinians face severe restrictions under military law. This disparity has contributed to a climate where human rights violations are prevalent, particularly against women and girls.

Israel's legal framework ostensibly supports human rights through various laws aimed at protecting women and girls. For instance, there are comprehensive laws addressing violence against women, including sexual harassment and trafficking. However, the implementation of these laws often falls short. Reports indicate that while legislation exists, enforcement is inconsistent, leading to inadequate protection for victims and insufficient accountability for perpetrators.

Specific incidents illustrate the human rights violations faced by Palestinian women and girls. Reports from international organizations detail cases of arbitrary detention, torture, and extrajudicial killings by Israeli forces. Testimonies highlight the psychological trauma inflicted on these individuals due to violence and discrimination, emphasizing the urgent need for accountability and reform.

Claims that Israel serves as a safe haven for pedophiles are supported by reports indicating that individuals with histories of sexual offenses have relocated to Israel, exploiting the Law of Return. This law allows Jews from around the world to immigrate to Israel with relative ease, but critics argue that it lacks adequate safeguards against those with criminal backgrounds. Activists have highlighted instances where offenders evade justice by relocating to Israel, raising concerns about public safety.

Mark Zuckerberg's Ownership of Beachfront Land In Hawaii

Mark Zuckerberg, born on May 14th 1984, is the co-founder and CEO of Facebook, now known as Meta Platforms, Inc. Since its inception in 2004, Facebook has grown to become one of the largest social media platforms globally, significantly impacting communication and social interaction. Zuckerberg's success has made him one of the wealthiest individuals in the world, leading to substantial investments in real estate, including over 1,300 acres of beachfront land in Hawaii.

Hawaii's land ownership carries profound historical significance, particularly concerning its indigenous population. The concept of land ownership in Hawaii is deeply intertwined with the culture and identity of Native Hawaiians. Historically, land was communally owned and managed under a system that respected the relationship between people and their environment. However, colonial practices disrupted this system, leading to significant loss of land and cultural dislocation for Native Hawaiians.

Zuckerberg's acquisition of beachfront properties began in 2014 when he purchased a 700 acre oceanfront property on Kauai for $100 million. This purchase marked the beginning of a series of acquisitions that would eventually lead him to control over 1,300 acres. The timeline of these acquisitions reflects a growing trend among wealthy individuals seeking to invest in Hawaii's real estate market.

The implications of such large scale land ownership by a single individual are significant. In Hawaiian culture, land is not merely a commodity; it is an integral part of identity and community. The consolidation of land ownership by billionaires raises concerns about the erosion of local culture and the rights of Native Hawaiians, who historically have been marginalized in discussions about land use and ownership.

In late 2016, Zuckerberg's team initiated quiet title lawsuits aimed at clarifying ownership disputes regarding small parcels of land within his estate. These lawsuits targeted land that had been owned by Native Hawaiians since the mid-19th century but had unclear titles due to historical complexities surrounding inheritance and property rights. The purpose of these lawsuits was to establish legal clarity over the ownership of these parcels, many of which were owned by multiple descendants unaware of their shares. However, this legal strategy faced backlash from local communities who viewed it as an attempt to further consolidate control over ancestral lands. Such actions exemplified a disregard for Native Hawaiian rights and contributed to ongoing patterns of neocolonialism.

The concept of neo-colonialism is central to understanding the implications of Zuckerberg's actions in Hawaii. Neo-colonialism refers to the continued economic and cultural dominance exerted by former colonial powers or wealthy individuals over indigenous populations. In this context, Zuckerberg's acquisition and legal maneuvers can be seen as a modern manifestation of colonial practices that prioritize profit over cultural heritage.

Perspectives from various stakeholders reveal a complex landscape of opinions regarding Zuckerberg's actions. Local residents and activists often view his land consolidation efforts as a continuation of historical injustices faced by Native Hawaiians. Legal experts emphasize the need for equitable solutions that respect indigenous rights while navigating contemporary property laws.

"We cannot let the world believe for a moment that this is a legitimate exercise of jurisdiction by the Court against Israel because to do so means we could be next."

U.S. Senator Lindsey Graham's response to ICC issuing an arrest warrant for war criminal **Prime Minister of Israel Benjamin Netanyahu**

Rising Down

Fait Accompli

YouTube

www.ingramcontent.com/pod-product-compliance
Lightning Source LLC
LaVergne TN
LVHW091204150826
845672LV00005B/1238

* 9 7 9 8 2 3 0 9 8 7 0 8 6 *